Gay Speir.
Christmas 2001

OLD FRIENDS AND MODERN INSTANCES

To Benjamin, Garrett and Marina

NICHOLAS HENDERSON

OLD FRIENDS AND MODERN INSTANCES

P

PROFILE BOOKS

First published in Great Britain in 2000 by
Profile Books Ltd
58A Hatton Garden
London ECIN 8LX
www.profilebooks.co.uk

Copyright © Nicholas Henderson, 2000

Typeset in Minion by MacGuru
info@macguru.org.uk

Designed by Peter Campbell

Printed and bound in Great Britain by
St Edmundsbury Press, Bury St Edmunds

A CIP catalogue record for this book is available from the British Library.

ISBN 1 86197 246 6

CONTENTS

ACKNOWLEDGEMENTS

I wish to thank the principal characters in each chapter for the information they have provided and for their forbearance in not asking to see the text in advance of publication.

I am greatly indebted to Margaret Chester for her expertise as a walking guidebook for authors, and for running through the whole text, making positive suggestions and hunting down solecisms.

I have also to thank the following for their agreement : (1) Hilary Spurling to my use of some of the material about Bloomsbury that was published in the *Charleston Magazine*; (2) Clive Aslet to the publication of my account of fishing with Cy Sulzberger in Kurdistan, a version of which appeared in *Country Life*; and (3) Richard Usborne to my publication here of part of an article about Julian Amery that was included in the book he edited, *A Century of Summer Fields*.

I am most grateful to the following for their insights into some of the people I have described: John Banham, John Birt, Terry Burns, Peter Carrington, Michael Charlton, Gay Charteris (née

Margesson), Kenneth Clarke, Nigel Clive, Geoffrey Cox, Prudence Davies, Robin Day, Paul Fox, Nicky Gordon-Lennox, John Grigg, Robert Haslam, Toby Henderson (my sister), Jeremy Isaacs, Kenneth James, Ludovic Kennedy, Nigel Lawson, Douglas McDougall, John Newton, Andrew Palmer, Roy Foster, John Roberts, Dadie Rylands, Peter Stothard, George Walden, Charles Wheeler, Alison Wright and David Wright.

I owe thanks for the help I have received in different ways from Mary (my wife), Alexandra (my daughter) and Marina (my granddaughter).

Finally, I have to say how grateful I am to Peter Carson of Profile Books. He gave me the idea for this book, helped me with many suggestions and has stuck with it throughout, even if the final outcome is rather different from his original proposal.

ILLUSTRATIONS

Acknowledgements: Lady Annan, p. 38; Lady Charteris, p. 2; Sir Howard Davies, p. 180; Duchess of Devonshire, p. 138; Mary Henderson, p. 106; Dame Jennifer Jenkins, p. 92; Robert Kee, p. 51, Countess of Longford, p. 62; Nigel Nicolson, p. 146; Mrs Frances Partridge, pp. 12, 17; QAPhotos, p. 160; Summer Fields, p. 30; Mrs Alison Wright, p. 82. The others are the author's.

PREFACE

This is a scrapbook of recollections triggered off by passing incidents. These may not have been important at the time and may well be thought today to show the characters concerned in a superficial and frivolous light. But I have noticed how frequently the clearest memory I have of someone I have known for a long time is connected with a particular and often an early occasion. I have also always been interested in how people seek pleasure and spend their spare time. None of this means that I underestimate the serious side of those I have depicted. Indeed, I have given a brief account of some of their lives and careers in order to provide a proper background against which these fleeting events may be seen.

Turning the pages of the past has been an eye-opener. Some of the glimpses have shown how social behaviour and attitudes have evolved in recent times; and this is particularly apparent, I think, in the piece about Howard Davies, who belongs to a different generation from the others I have described. No underlying theme connects my portraits, and the only link is my presence.

Accounts of people and events prominent in my official life have not been included here as these have been recorded in my two autobiographical publications, *The Private Office* and *Mandarin.*

Footnotes are given to the main characters in the chapters. Brief details of others mentioned are provided in the Index with Notes.

1

LESSONS IN BLOOMSBURY

She peered at me, a little frighteningly, through thick pebble-glasses. Her voice rose to a high pitch as she insisted that what she was explaining was 'perfectly obvious'. She stressed the first syllable of the words in what I later realised was the idiosyncratic Bloomsbury intonation. As if to give greater emphasis to her instruction, her face came close up to mine and with it also came a showery accompaniment.

I was being taught to read at Charleston by Marjorie Strachey[1], the youngest sister of Lytton. She ran a small school for the children of her Bloomsbury friends. In the winter it met in Gordon Square in the house occupied by members of the Strachey family; in the summer it moved to Charleston, the house on the Sussex Downs where Vanessa and Clive Bell and Duncan Grant lived and where they entertained members of the Bloomsbury circle. My mother knew many of them and was a close friend of

---

1 Marjorie Strachey, 1882–1964, the youngest of Lytton Strachey's five sisters, all of whom were older than him. He had three older brothers and one younger.

*Marjorie Strachey
playing in a chess
tournament.*

Lytton and Carrington. My own close contact at the time was
with Angelica Bell, Vanessa's daughter. We were so attached that
we became known, in the jargon of the school, as 'sticky friends'.
We spent much time together in a tree-house we built in the top
of a row of limes.

I think we children were influenced for the rest of our lives by
the beauty of Charleston – by the decorations on the walls and
doors and on all the furniture, by the walled garden with its statuary and by the setting in the Downs. This peaceful idyll was apt
to be disturbed by a periodic drama that kept us all on the *qui
vive*. This occurred when the cows from the adjacent farm would
wander into the pond outside the house, would become stuck in
the mud and would have to be extricated by the farm hands who

accompanied their heaving with much loud and descriptive shouting. The pond was regarded by us children as a danger area, not merely for the cows but for ourselves, as Baba Anrep, who was older than the rest of us, would entice us to climb along the branch of an overhanging willow tree which she would then shake so that we were in danger of falling off into the muddy water.

Marjorie Strachey loved teaching and though I was certainly in awe of those piercing eyes and those strident chords, I was swept along in the current of her enthusiasm. Quentin Bell has described her as 'a teacher of genius'. Marjorie's punishment was to send us to 'prison' as she called it, which meant being made to stand in silence in the corner of her sitting-room while she carried on a lively conversation with such friends as Clive Bell, Duncan Grant and Roger Fry. It was punishment which I recall with gratitude. Without understanding the significance of much that was said, I was conscious of the way this circle of friends discussed ideas and generalisations, and did so with heat and enthusiasm, besides relishing the exchange of gossip and criticism about each other.

After running this small Bloomsbury school, Marjorie became the private tutor of the Margesson family. When they moved to the country she moved with them and lived in a cottage a few yards from their house. Discussion of Marjorie with the Margessons in later years formed a close bond between us. They were inspired by her as we had been. When she read *Hamlet* to them for the first time she closed the book after the opening scene where the ghost of Hamlet's father appears on the castle battlements and said: 'What do you think of that as the beginning of a play?'

It was not only English literature that she loved but French too. She had been educated by a remarkable French woman, Mademoiselle Souvestre, among whose other pupils had been Eleanor Roosevelt. Marjorie adored reading out the plays of Racine and would impart Gallic emotion and drama to her audience.

For the Margessons, being taught maths by her was something of an ordeal. She minded intensely when they made a silly mistake. 'You're quite mad,' she would say before raising her voice to add: 'You must be out of your mind,' followed by 'You're a complete cretin,' and ending with a despairing groan. Marjorie said on some occasion to one of the Margesson girls: 'You will think it very remarkable one day that I could teach you every subject.' She did not then but she has since.

Their mother, Frances Margesson, also became part of Marjorie's school, as did one or two other children of neighbouring families. Over lunch they discussed literature and music. Byron and Keats were favourite topics. She pounced on any trite remark. Mrs Margesson once remarked that she didn't like Mozart. She received a stern reply: 'My dear, you don't know him.'

The chief sport of the Margesson girls was riding and one day Marjorie, who had never ridden in her life and was by then in her late forties, announced that she would like to take up riding. A quiet pony was found, strong enough to take her considerable weight, and Marjorie joined the family ride, lamenting that she had so few years left in which to enjoy this new activity.

Her favourite pastime was chess, which she taught to her maid who was the daughter of the publican in the nearby village. For many years chess tournaments were held in the pub.

Yes, Marjorie had a maid then; but not later in the war years when she lived in London. To her former pupils she lamented her lack of skill in housework, explaining that she had to make her own bed and felt so tired after doing so that she had to get back into it to recover.

An example of Marjorie's unquenchable desire to instruct came my way several decades later when she was staying with us in Vienna where I was serving as first secretary in the British Embassy. We took her to see a Shakespeare play at the Burgtheater. In the interval at the bar she began discussing the meaning and merits of the play, expressing her views loudly and categorically. She was soon the centre of attention and by the time the interval ended she had gathered a large audience, all of whom were listening with close attention, and many of whom seemed reluctant to return to their seats to hear the Bard's own words.

The pedagogic instincts that possessed Marjorie extended to the giving of worldly advice. She told me that she could help me with a tip in case I ever found difficulty in my diplomatic life in engaging someone in conversation. 'What you should do', she said, 'is to ask them about distances. Ask them how far it is from X to Y. You will find that it breaks the ice.' I sometimes reflected on this when having a sticky conversational time at some official function in Paris, but decided that if I adopted Marjorie's wheeze I could well be met with the realistic Gallic response that I should take a look at Michelin.

Bloomsbury had a reputation for disliking children; they were regarded with almost as much antipathy as were dogs. At least that was the theory. But I cannot say that that was my experience, though I was aware of their reputed hostility, which only made their presence more exciting. The reading lessons with Marjorie, like the drawing instruction I received from Vanessa Bell and the attention during frequent amateur theatricals from Duncan Grant and others in that closed circle, created in me a life-long feeling of warmth and gratitude towards them.

Children at Charleston were looked after by one or more of the Selwoods, a family that should feature in any prosopography of Bloomsbury. The Selwood parents had a very small farm in the hamlet of Oldown, which stood on a hill above the village of Tockington, not far from Bristol. The family were discovered for Bloomsbury by Dadie Rylands, whose parents lived nearby. My two sisters and I went for holidays to stay with them. We called them 'Mother' and 'Dad' which was how we saw them. Dad had been a groom, Mother the village dressmaker. We spent hours in the farmyard which was as near to paradise as I have ever lived. Everything worthwhile seemed to go on there. We fed the chickens and the pigs. We collected the eggs. We groomed and helped harness the pony before setting off in the trap with Dad.

The domestic and nursery services of one or other of the seven Selwood sisters enabled many of the Bloomsbury parents who employed them to lead relatively carefree lives as regards the upbringing of their children. I don't recall Mabel or Flossie or Marion or Daisy or any of the other Selwoods expressing surprise, let alone criticism, over the somewhat unconventional lifestyle of some of their employers. Unquestioningly loyal, they took everything in their broad Selwood stride. One of the sisters had an illegitimate daughter who was brought up with us.

At Charleston during the summers Vanessa and Duncan allowed us into their studio, which to a child had a magical quality.

It was full of half-finished portraits, furniture in the process of being painted, large Spanish plates and jugs, easels, multi-coloured palettes, brushes – all the alluring accoutrements of an artist's life. I had never been in a studio before. Vanessa painted my portrait there, and it seemed to me, though as a child I would not have put it in those terms, that in the process we struck up some sort of a relationship. I often talked about her many years later when I was seeing members of the Euston Road school of artists. She invited me to Charleston for Angelica's twenty-first birthday party and although the spell of the place could not be re-captured I felt a certain rapport with Vanessa springing from our earlier friendship.

Vanessa's sister, Virginia Woolf, was a fleeting but friendly presence in the children's world at Charleston or in Gordon Square. She took much trouble with her nieces, Ann and Judith Stephen. Ann described Virginia as 'the ideal aunt', perhaps be-cause she would take her to the opera, such as *The Magic Flute* or *Die Fledermaus,* after first treating her to supper in the Woolfs' house in Tavistock Square. Ann recounted how Leonard's hand shook alarmingly as he carved the joint, giving the best slices to his red spaniel, Pinker.

We children were sometimes invited to Bloomsbury's parties in Gordon Square or in a studio in Fitzroy Square. They were rol-licking. Duncan danced like the proverbial dervish, dressed in elaborate or, more often, scanty costume. Lydia Keynes was a con-spicuous guest at these parties. Her reputation as a dancer was more glamorous to us than Maynard's as an economist. But while abandoned enough in the *pas de deux* she performed with Dun-can, her figure was memorably dumpy compared with his. At one party Lydia sang a song beginning: 'My earrings, my earrings, I have dropped them in the well,' while Rachel MacCarthy acted very prettily in a Victorian dress; and her mother, dressed in deep disguise, told fortunes. The young sang for their supper by acting in little plays written especially for them. Invariably seated in the front row, Clive Bell encouraged us with loud laughter and hearty applause. He was usually the author of the plays.

I only kept intermittently in touch with Bloomsbury in later life, but half a century after the events I am describing here Duncan asked if he could stay with us in Paris, where I was ambassador. He wanted to see an exhibition of Cézanne, his favourite painter. It soon became apparent that, by now over ninety, he was living in the past. We gave a dinner party for him at which he wore a voluminous shawl and an enormous hat. He had the frustrated anger of old age which was in stark contrast to the benign disposition that I remember he had as a young man. Early in the evening he summoned me peremptorily and, pointing to one of the *grandes dames* present asked ferociously: 'What is Ottoline Morrell doing here?'

Soon after Mary and I were married, Vanessa invited us to a party in Gordon Square where we met another of Lytton's sisters, Madame Bussy. We asked her if she would like to come to tea with us one day, to which she replied by asking where we lived. When we said 'Knightsbridge,' she expostulated: 'So far from Bloomsbury.'

My upbringing in the Bloomsbury milieu came to an end when I was still very young because my father disapproved of it. He was gentle and kind but had distinct dislikes, or at any rate prejudices. Academically brilliant, and politically involved – as a

Liberal – he had few cultural interests except literature, and he did not feel at home in the Bloomsbury circle. He was Scottish, very Scottish in his lack of caprice and sensuality. While not at all quarrelsome by nature, I do not think that he was on easy terms with Leonard Woolf, who ran the book pages of *The Nation*, a paper of which Maynard Keynes made my father the editor in the twenties. My father was a close friend of Maynard; indeed a partner, and one of the few in the specialist world of economics at the time who, so I was told, was on equal sparring terms with the master. But this did not endear Bloomsbury to him.

My mother maintained contact with her old friends and acquired a cottage in the country near Hamspray House to be near them. Thanks to that connection, I was able, as a child, to see something of the people and life of that other great downland stable of Bloomsbury.

2

THE TWO CHATELAINES
OF HAMSPRAY

Carrington[1] arrived on horseback after riding across the downs
from Hamspray. She was living there with Lytton Strachey and
her husband, Ralph Partridge, a triangle that received much publicity in later years. Hamspray was a Georgian house looking
across fields to the Berkshire Downs, upon which grew a dense
row of beeches called the Bull's Tail from the way they followed
the descending gradient of the hill. Along the front of the house
stood a glass-roofed verandah.

This was Carrington's first visit to the cottage which my
mother, a great friend of hers, had recently bought so as to be
near her. She was wearing riding-breeches which were of a cut
that, even to my young, unclothes-conscious eye, did not appear
smart, but that did seem to me to have a certain style. The same
might have been said of her appearance, at any rate as it seemed
to me then: she did not have the beauty or elegance of the film

---

1 Dora Houghton Carrington, 1893–1932, painter, muse of Lytton Strachey, m.
Ralph Partridge.

Carrington at Hamspray.

stars or society ladies whose photos I admired in the papers; and there was something tomboyish about her mop of hair, the puzzled expression in her strikingly blue eyes, her walk and movements and the way she stood with toes turned in. She was distinctive and a little defenceless and very different from the other grown-ups whom I was accustomed to meet. Perhaps it was this last quality that attracted me to her.

Her grey mare, called Belle, had been a present for her, purchased by Lytton from the butcher in Hungerford, and she loved it, as she wrote later, 'more than any man, but less than some women'. It had a clumsy trot that belied its name. Carrington allowed me to ride Belle even though I was only eleven and had never had any lessons in horsemanship. It was not long before I was badly thrown, which led me to give up riding. I have to record, in mitigation of my ineptitude, that Carrington revealed the mare's unsureness of foot in a letter to the writer Gerald Brenan, recounting how she was thrown by her, falling on the steep road down Ham Hill.

Instead of riding, therefore, I took to eavesdropping on Carrington's conversations with my mother. I know I was intrigued by them and, even if I can't remember specifically anything that was said, I do recall how intensely they chatted. In a letter to Lytton Strachey, Carrington wrote of my mother at this time: 'Faith seems in high spirits and is very charming ... she is a regular old gossip, but I am very wary and glean more than she reaps.' Carrington had a special way of speaking. She had to a marked degree the Bloomsbury intonation, and the practice of stressing as important something that in those days was not usually thought to be so, saying for instance about some couple, 'extraordinary people, they're married'. She often seemed a little out of breath. From time to time she would give a slight shake of her fringe which, like the rest of her hair, had the colour and density of thatch; and she would frequently lick her lips as she and my mother sipped cherry brandy. This seemed to be one of the favourite tipples of Bloomsbury at this time and my mother used to drive into Newbury, ahead of Carrington's visits, to buy a bottle of the liqueur, made, as I then clearly registered, by the Danish firm, Heering. This may explain in Proustian fashion, I suppose, the love I have always had since childhood for Heering's Cherry Brandy.

I think that it was from listening to these conversations, and from my mother's highly individual elaborations afterwards, that

I first sensed the ethos of Bloomsbury: the contempt for received opinions and conventionality; the disdain for philistines – a favourite term of reproach; the enthronement of reason over spirituality; the readiness of men and women to discuss everything together without inhibition; the enthusiasm for creativity; the dislike of pomposity and humbug; the lack of interest in popularity; and, not least noticeable, if rarely cited later as an essential characteristic of the group, their sense of fun, so that humour and laughter constantly sparkled in their world.

During the course of many visits Carrington did some lovely paintings in our cottage – over the doors, round the fireplaces and above the chimney-piece, details of which were given in Jane Hill's catalogue to the 1995 exhibition of Carrington's work at the Barbican. Alas, they have been painted over by later owners. In a letter to Gerald Brenan she wrote: 'Faith says she likes her decorated cottage which is a good thing', adding in words that to us in this telecommunication age may sound a little quaint, 'She rang me up on the telephone.'

Carrington gave my mother a painting of dahlias which now hangs in our house in London. She did much decoration in Hamspray and everything she did bore her unmistakable stamp even if she never signed any of her paintings. Paper lampshades painted for some party were still there some thirty years later. Frances Partridge[1], who succeeded her as chatelaine of Hamspray, wrote of her pictures that 'they showed an immense natural talent which perhaps never matured'. This is faint praise and I have to

---

1 Frances Partridge, CBE, b. 1900, d. of W. C. Marshall, architect; translator from French and German, author, literary journalist, m. Ralph Partridge 1933, one son, Burgo, d. 1963.

say that, for me, it is precisely the almost child-like quality of Carrington's pictures that holds much of their charm. I was very conscious of her intense feeling for the countryside near Hamspray where she had been brought up. I bought a cottage there many years later and have always had in my mind's eye the image of her painting of the nearby hill at Hurstbourne Tarrant. Love for a work of art can attract you to the artist; and I have certainly come to be increasingly drawn to Carrington by my feeling for her paintings.

In Lytton Strachey's time, children were not invited to Hamspray. *Le petit peuple*, he called them in a scarcely flattering tone. The reputation of being anti-children that Bloomsbury earned, and made no effort to disavow, owed a lot to him. A pram in the hall at Hamspray would have been unimaginable in his day. However, after his death and Carrington's and when Frances was living there with Ralph, a pram bearing their son, Burgo, soon made its appearance; and we children became frequent visitors.

For those not steeped in the annals of Bloomsbury, I should explain here how this change of watch from Carrington to Frances came about. By the mid-twenties Ralph's relations with Carrington had deteriorated, though he could not get her out of his system. As he confided to Rosamond Lehmann, 'once she got into anybody's blood she was ineradicable'. He and Frances fell in love. They spent the weekends at Hamspray, where Carrington remained the chatelaine and where Lytton was often present. Carrington was in love with Lytton, though not sexually, and he with her in the same way. Lytton had been in love with, and remained devoted to, Ralph. He was determined that the Hamspray set-up, a somewhat lop-sided *ménage à trois*, or if it had to be, *à quatre*, should endure and should not, therefore, be disturbed, as it would inevitably be if, for instance, Ralph divorced Carrington to marry Frances. He had his way and the ménage continued until, in 1932, Lytton died. Following his death, Carrington committed suicide as she felt unable to live without him. Frances then became chatelaine of Hamspray.

Reflecting from today's standpoint on the unconventional private lives of Bloomsbury, it is astonishing how private they remained – until the disclosures detonated a generation later by Michael Holroyd in his biography of Lytton. Many of the leading members – Maynard Keynes, Virginia Woolf and Lytton, for instance – were widely known and revered for their work, but little percolated to the public at large about their unorthodox life-style. This was, of course, partly because homosexuality was illegal; but it also reflected the restraint of the press and the respect for privacy that prevailed at the time, not just in Bloomsbury. No less striking and relevant was the scathing attitude of Bloomsbury to the pursuit of publicity, let alone popularity. They did not want to be household names. They did not exactly seek anonymity or shun the admiration of those who escaped the stigma of being philistines – the élite in modern parlance, not that that was a term in as current use then as today. No doubt it helped that many members of Bloomsbury had some private means and did not therefore have to curry favour in the market place. But, more important, I believe, was the markedly unmercenary ethos of their world, as indeed of the middle class as a whole in the UK at that time.

Many of the customs and attitudes of Bloomsbury – e.g. their lack of inhibitions about discussing everything in mixed com-

*Frances Marshall (Partridge)
with Duncan Grant, late
twenties.*

pany, their openness about homosexuality, and their readiness to
'live in sin', as they called it, regardless of the frown of conventional opinion – these have become so commonplace today as to
make it easy to overlook how considerable was Bloomsbury's part
in bringing about changes in social mores.

The first and most lasting image I have of Frances at this stage
is of her diving and swimming. She and Ralph often took us with
them to a large, natural pool they had discovered in the area of
water meadows between Newbury and Kintbury where the river
Kennet and the canal run in parallel. The Cornish Riviera Express
went whizzing closely by on the Great Western line and, emerging

from the water, we waved, as was a customary salutation in those days to passing steam trains. Frances was in the habit of diving from a bridge and I saw her like the cormorant in my book of sea birds. Watching her then and when she was playing badminton at Hamspray I was astonished by her athleticism. I would not have been so amazed had I known then what I only discovered later, that her father had been a finalist in the first men's singles at Wimbledon in 1877; and that she had been a first-rate ballroom dancer in her early twenties. At Cambridge she danced regularly with Lord Louis Mountbatten. At Bloomsbury parties she danced skilfully and passionately the blues, the Charleston and the Black Bottom. She was runner-up one year in the world dancing championship at Queen's Hall.

We would also be invited to Hamspray for tea and to swim in their tiny pool. It was obligatory to bathe naked, which was all very well if you had the magnificent torso of Ralph or the beautiful figure of Frances, or, I suppose, our children's bodies.

There was nothing perfunctory about tea at Hamspray: we sat round the table in the dining-room; we ate home-made cakes and jam; and we took part in general conversation. Talk was often of ideas. As I have already mentioned, Bloomsbury had a reputation for discussing everything, regardless of the company, whether it was about infidelity, passion or sex of all kinds. After all, James Strachey, Lytton's brother, who was often to be seen seated in a deck-chair on the lawn at Hamspray during weekends, was Freud's main English translator. I can't remember having been shocked by anything said during these tea-parties. Probably I was too young and innocent to be shockable.

Mention was sometimes made of the *Greville Memoirs* describing court and aristocratic life at the end of the eighteenth and beginning of the nineteenth centuries, which Ralph and Frances had helped to edit, annotate and index. The literary pages of the *New Statesman* were also a favourite topic: Cyril Connolly was condemned for an article in which he had listed all the subjects that should be taboo in a modern novel. He would have come in for more than condemnation had they known at Hamspray how he dubbed Ralph the Berkshire Bull. Their critical faculties were well developed in the Bloomsbury tradition, not least in discussing each other's works, but this did not prevent enthusiasm, particularly for the undiscovered, the creative or the unconventional. Their conversation was apt to be interlarded with French words or expressions, noticeably when enthusiasm was being shown. People were often described as *dégagé* in their character or *hors concours* in their achievement.

Ralph regularly reviewed detective stories in the *New Statesman*. We would ask him whether in the latest Agatha Christie he had guessed who the murderer was; and he would explain his technique for picking up real clues rather than red herrings. He had a gift for analysis and description, whether applied to his friends, to literature, to the game of cricket or to the inhabitants of Broadmoor about whom he wrote a book.

In later life, Frances came to resent the unflattering way Ralph was often described in the many books published about Bloomsbury. It was as if these tried to achieve a chiaroscuro effect by contrasting the brawniness of Ralph with the braininess of his Bloomsbury friends. To me as a child, Ralph's record as a scholar and an athlete was impressive, and I was aware of how his experiences in the war had led to his insistence upon leading a peaceful and uneventful life afterwards. I was also the beneficiary of his personal kindness. He took me on several expeditions to look for plovers' eggs in the vast hundred-acre field by the village of Combe over the downs. Equipped with field glasses, we would watch closely where a bird landed and we would then observe it as it ran along to its nest that was camouflaged in the flinty surface of the ground. Without taking our eyes off the spot where it settled we would walk straight towards it to collect the eggs. We didn't seem to think there was anything wrong in those days in taking plovers' eggs.

Jigsaw puzzles were a speciality of the house. A half-finished one invariably lay scattered upon a table and Frances would implore us to help complete 'the beastly thing'. This was difficult because the puzzles were not the usual interlocking type with sharply contrasted colours, but came from a library which specialised in pictures that were almost monochrome and in pieces that were so cut as to give no clue to where they were to be fitted. These jigsaws were of the same teasingly difficult kind as the crosswords which were another concomitant of Hamspray life. The *Times* crossword was always polished off quickly. The puzzles they liked best were those set by Torquemada in the *Observer*. Flatteringly, we would occasionally be asked to help with some clue, perhaps a quotation; but of course it was absurd to think we could do better than Frances, who has remained a crossword-maestro all her life.

The presence of Saxon Sydney Turner forms a landmark on my memory map of Hamspray. He was a frequent weekender, whether in the time of Carrington or of Frances Partridge. The parabola of his career was legendary: the most brilliant scholar of his day at Cambridge, he had passed top into the Treasury, where he remained for the rest of his official life, achieving promotion only once, whether because of his ability to see all sides of a question and hence his inability ever to make up his mind upon any problem submitted to him, or, as some of his many Bloomsbury friends averred, on account of his reluctance to vacate his room at the Treasury, which had a beautiful view. He was very silent and not given to expressing his views, a reticence that differentiated him from most of the company.

Saxon communicated with us children in grunts, in quite friendly noises like 'umph'. He wore dark-blue shirts. He smoked a pipe, as did Ralph and another frequent visitor, Clive Bell, a favourite of Frances. Saxon never married but nursed an undying passion for my aunt, Barbara Bagenal, a contemporary of Carrington at the Slade, to whom, so we were led to believe, he was generous to a fault – a pet phrase in that circle – giving her large boxes of chocolates and taking her frequently to the opera, never missing a performance of *The Ring* at Covent Garden. When I was old enough, Saxon invited me to his club in London where, after dinner, we played chess, a game he invariably won.

The painter Joan Souter-Robertson, or Joan Cochemé, as she later became, was another regular guest at Hamspray. She could not help seducing the young as well as the old. Her white-peach complexion, her small but voluptuous figure, her ready way of laughing as though she had a sweet in her mouth, and her habit of saying complimentary things – these qualities made her the irresistible flirt of Bloomsbury. Her paintings of flower markets and small ships in tiny harbours were easy for the young to relate to. Later she specialised in painting children.

Boris Anrep, the mosaicist, had been one of Joan's admirers, but then, as my mother used to say, he was very susceptible to the opposite sex and was never content to have just one woman in his life at any one time. He much admired Frances, but in a different way from Joan Cochemé.

One summer day at Hamspray when Boris was staying there, speculation started about who was larger round the chest, he or Ralph. A tape was produced and they stood on the lawn while measurements were taken. I don't recall who was the winner, but I know I was surprised that there should have been a competition at all, as I was aware of Ralph's magnificent build, having seen him bathing. Boris did not strike me as a heavy man. He was a keen tennis and ping-pong player, and eager to win at both, as I discovered when years later I played with him in his club in Paris. In appearance and movement he seemed like a large yet agile animal, as he padded about in his loose-fitting trousers, shaggy jacket and exaggeratedly square-toed shoes, characteristics that inevitably appealed to me when, very young, I first set eyes upon him. His speech had the charm that all Russians have when they speak English. He pronounced 'th' as 'f', so that he always called my mother 'Faif', which I thought sympathetic. Frances's memory of him is kept warm by the mosaic fire-surround depicting a cat that she has installed in the apartment in London where she has since lived.

From any account of Hamspray in those years, however brief, the question inevitably arises about the nature of the relationship between the two chatelaines: how did they manage to get along? Their characters were theatrically contrasted: Carrington was devious (Ralph's word for her), elusive, capricious, inventive, unacademically minded, sceptical of all conventional human bonds, flirtatious and desirous of the enchantments of love while worried about her own sexuality (she hated being a woman), and attracted as much to women as to men. 'I believe I am a perfect combination of a nymphomaniac and a wood-nymph,' she wrote to Lytton. 'I hanker after intimacies which another side of my nature is perpetually at war against.'

By comparison Frances was normal and uncomplicated. She was realistic, dependable and intellectual. She had strong opinions, notably on pacifism, and was fond of discussing ideas. She was faithful while tolerant of the infidelity of others. Her life was governed by the pursuit of truth.

Yet it would be a travesty of this truth if I were to give the impression that she was unfeeling or that her life had been one long process of calculation without regard to the feelings of others. Of her other strong impulses she has said: 'I am a hedonist and I have always been visually orientated.' From visits to the Lake District as a child she discovered the intense pleasure she could get from the natural world 'which is still one of my strongest emotions'.

It is something of a relief that someone so reasonable and so balanced should have strong intolerances or prejudices as well as passionate pleasures. Excessive drink, the display of great wealth, reliance on conventionality or privilege – these are her dislikes; but if this makes her sound priggish I must correct it by emphasising that she is a great enjoyer, a lover of wild flowers, food, conversation and, not least, travel.

Running into her at some party just before her ninety-first birthday and telling her that we were about to go on a package tour to Cyprus, I said to her casually, 'I suppose you wouldn't like to come?' To which she replied immediately, 'You know I'm a very "Yes" person.' She accepted and came and kept all the other travellers informed and enchanted with her knowledge of the island's wild flowers.

In *Lytton Strachey*, Michael Holroyd has described how awkward, how unenjoyable, were Frances's visits to Hamspray when Carrington was there: 'Both Lytton and Carrington saw her as a potential danger to their way of life – for all her excellent qualities, she was not really their type of person: too unrealistically straightforward and remorselessly well balanced.' Ralph was uneasy also, realising how out of it Frances must feel. Frances was aware of the strong obstacle to their happiness together that was created, as she expressed it, 'by the combination of Lytton, Carrington and Hamspray'. Even the house appeared to have entered into the already complicated relationship. Yet no one was prepared to walk off stage. Promiscuous though she was, Carrington was not in the habit of ever giving anyone up. Frances did not see why she should give up Ralph; they were both in love. She had also come to feel that she belonged to the Bloomsbury world. When she had first entered it she felt 'as if a lot of doors had suddenly opened out of a stuffy room'.

Surprisingly, perhaps, Frances and Carrington had respect for each other: Frances recognised the streak of genius in Carrington. Carrington, as was her wont, had moments of great affection for Frances. 'I am very fond of you,' she wrote to her. Nevertheless, both must have wished the other out of the way. It could not surely have lasted much longer without ending in tragedy. This occurred, and in a most unexpected way, with the fatal but undiagnosed cancer of the one person who had been the least affected by the drama, Lytton. His untimely death in 1932 and Carring-ton's suicide soon after were sad indeed but they brought the long-running drama to an end. Carrington left a note for Ralph saying that she hoped he would marry Frances and that they would have children. Ralph and Frances married the following year and lived happily at Hamspray until Ralph died in 1960. Their son Burgo died tragically only a few years later.

It was typical of Frances's acceptance of reality and of her lack of vainglory that when she moved into Hamspray she refrained from altering the decoration of the house which remained very much as Carrington had left it. That was how Ralph wanted it, be-sides which, as she shared the taste of the house, she saw no rea-son for change. She left her stamp on Hamspray in a different way. She made it a sanctuary for friendships; and she regarded the practice of friendship as somewhere between art and love.

With her gift for the description of everyday things and of the characters of the visitors, she has left in her diaries an invaluable record of the life that was led there. The diary also portrays her talent for simile which, for me, is a distinguishing feature of her writing. Speaking of a close friend, Raymond Mortimer, she says he was 'darting after pleasure and intellectual stimulus like a dragon-fly'. She writes of a 'Russian Easter cake stuck all over with almonds like a porcupine'. Or, to give another example, she asks the reader to think of the crowds who rush to a street accident 'like wasps to jam'.

Frances's reaction to death and bereavement have been the opposite of Carrington's. Ralph's death was for her a 'mortal blow', to use her own words about it; but, as if to confound this, she decided that suicide was not her way out. It would be selfish and cause pain to others. Her watchword for survival was 'Fill every moment'. Unhappiness, she believes, has to find an outlet whereas 'happiness enfolds one like a warm rug in silence'. So she applied herself to translating, writing her diary and friendships. She found solace in contemplating nature as in a walk by a stream. For others, her companionship has afforded an example of how the life-instinct can triumph over adversity.

Her friends have watched confidently as the years have rolled by and Frances, with but a slight impairment of her faculties, noticeable only in her reduced sight and nimbleness, has needed to make few concessions to old age. She has continued to live alone, look after herself, write, entertain, travel and go for walks.

When she rounded Millennium Corner and entered the home straight to her one-hundredth birthday which fell on 15 March 2000, it was possible to detect in her a slight frisson. By a short head she was leading the Queen Mother, who was due to reach her centenary a few months later. She began to receive increased media attention, which she didn't mind when it was concerned with her writings or with her role as the last survivor of the Bloomsbury Group. On the contrary, in her realistic way, she was rather tickled by it and even flattered, as she was by the award of the CBE, which she, unlike many members of Bloomsbury in earlier times who scoffed at such honours, was happy to receive from the Queen at Buckingham Palace in February. What she disliked was the impression some press stories were apt to convey that, on account of her longevity, she was some sort of freak, when in fact she felt herself to be completely normal.

Among the qualities that had most conspicuously endured was her gift of friendship. The living proof of this was demonstrated, as if in a *tableau vivant*, at her one-hundredth birthday party, given in the ballroom of the Savile, which was attended by some 150 of her friends. Few knew everyone, but, judging by the strains of revelry, none felt a stranger. They were united communally by the Bloomsbury connection and most of all, of course, by their friendship with Frances. The sound, ringing in my ears like a nursery rhyme, of the names of some of those at the party – Bell, Garnett, Anrep, Keynes, Gathorne-Hardy and Strachey – took me back to the days at Hamspray where I had first known Frances; and when, after several hours, I heard her say to someone who suggested that perhaps it was time to leave, 'But the party is still in full swing,' it occurred to me that the same could well be said of her.

3

MY FIRST CABINET MEETING

At the end of one Michaelmas term at our prep school, Summer Fields, Oxford, Julian Amery[1] invited me to spend the first day of the holidays with him in London. While most of the boys in the train to Paddington talked about the musical shows they were going to see, or read the *Daily Express*, or conceivably the *Morning Post*, Julian, then not thirteen, sat in a corner of the carriage reading *The Times*. By the time we arrived he was fully briefed.

His mother was at the station to meet us. She had a porter and a taxi ready. This, and everything else about her, suggested a sense of joyful expectation, as if this was the moment she had long been waiting for, the return of the beloved son from exile. In addition to showing clearly her own affectionate feelings, she managed to suggest that a number of other people in London had been yearning for this moment too: it was a public as well as a family occasion.

1 Lord Amery, 1919–1996, politician and author, son of Leopold Amery; on active service WW2, Egypt, Palestine and Adriatic; Minister of Civil Aviation, Minister of Public Building and Works and for Housing and Construction; Minister of State, FCO.

Julian Amery (in front) at Summer Fields, c. 1930.

We drove to their large house in Eaton Square in time for lunch. The vast dining-room seemed to consist of nothing but four enormous dark corners. Even at midday artificial light was needed. Julian's father, Leopold Amery, at that time in the middle of his political career, joined us and with his arrival began my first experience of a Cabinet meeting. Elaborately courteous though he was in his preliminaries, enquiring about Oxford and the Great Western Railway, he manifestly wanted to get down to the political agenda as soon as possible, which is what Julian also wanted.

There were only four of us round the table, two not yet in their teens, the other two over forty, but all of us alike in the urgent desire to work out together the burning problems facing England and the Empire – yes, Empire, for that was a word spoken loudly and frequently in that household, and, as can be imagined, the term 'Imperial Preference' did not go unbandied. Julian's father spoke authoritatively and at some length about the Locarno Treaty and the world economic situation. He was out of office at the time, but he gave the impression of really being in control of events, as if the others had merely managed to usurp temporarily the seats of power which would shortly be returned to their rightful guardians. It was my first experience of that 'we' and 'us' in which an earlier generation of Tories invariably embraced their audience, as though any other address would be unthinkable, and even insulting. At any rate, as the butler ceremoniously served the four of us, Mr Amery, including me instinctively in the fold, asked courteously for my views on the measures he had outlined for meeting the major international problems of the hour. Young though I was, I realised that I was there not to sing, but to listen for my supper. With a blush and a fumble for words, I passed the ball rapidly to Julian who, needless to say, was waiting for it. He took it gratefully and made off at a steady, confident pace which he maintained, with pauses only for suggestions of historical parallels, until coffee and brandy were handed round with marked formality, and the meeting ended. I do not recall what Julian said on the great issues of the day. I know that he was not exactly arguing against his father. It was more as though he was combining with him in the face of some unmentionable enemy. He seemed completely *au fait* with the problems, and gave the impression of having thought a lot about them during the tiresome interval of term-time which he had been forced to spend away from London.

Politics were the main business of his life; all the rest was a digression. There was nothing false about this. Julian's manner was pompous. We called him 'Pompo' at school, but this was because he was so different from the rest of us, so much more serious and self-assured. He was precisely what he claimed to be, a real, forth-right, mature politician who was already of seasoned Cabinet timber.

We had a debate at school on the subject of conscription. This was at the time – in the early 1930s – when pacifism was *de rigueur* in the schools and universities of England. The case for pacifism, or at any rate for 'voluntariness', had been put confidently by several of the senior, popular and athletic boys, who clearly had most of the audience behind them. Julian then rose to challenge the prevailing wind. He can only have been about eleven years old. He was small, pale and most unmilitary-looking. His hair shone with brilliantine in the evening lights of the debating-room. With one hand on the lapel of his jacket and the other clutching his notes, he began his speech in a voice quavering with age rather than youth, the vowels flat and repressed: 'Mr President, I am in favour of conscription. I've been in favour of conscription all my life …'

Julian was by nature defiant, but he was not rebellious in the normal adolescent fashion of resenting all authority. In fact he seemed to like authority, provided he had some say in it. He was founder and chairman of the Anti-Authority League, whose main purpose was to challenge the right of the masters to tell us how to organise our spare time. Julian's views, though invariably expressed with the gravitas of an elder statesman, were often unorthodox and inconsistent. He swung between right and left. At one moment he was a fervent admirer of Lloyd George, which did not endear him to most of the masters, and succeeded with pride in securing from the author a signed copy of *We Can Conquer Unemployment*. He was unfashionably in favour of strong men.

He used to talk much about 'Winston', in the same familiar way as the rest of us spoke of the cricketers Gubby (Allen) or Donald (Bradman). His chief hero was Napoleon Buonaparte. He usually had a biography of him handy, and he frequently thrust his right arm into his coat across his chest in what he assured us was Napoleon's style.

A faint aura of 'foreignness' hung about Julian. He spoke French perfectly, which annoyed us only a little more than it did the master from the Antipodes who taught us French. He scorned the use of a French-English dictionary, insisting that all that was needed was a Larousse. He talked much of strange capitals, giving the impression that his holidays were spent in *wagons-lits.* His spiritual home seemed to be the Balkans, a place that meant little to most of us, though to him it was both real and entrancing. Even the inhabitants – Serbs, Croats and Macedonians – he appeared to find tolerable. In this he did not have the rest of us with him.

He was uninhibitedly devoted to his parents in a demonstrative, scarcely English way. He did not exactly show them off, but he was uniquely unashamed of them, and was apparently quite unabashed to be seen kissing them and being kissed by them in public. This happened at half-term when they arrived by taxi and we all watched as they stepped out slowly to hug him and be hugged by him. Then the three of them – all more or less the same size – would climb into the cab without any sign of nervous flurry, and drive off, no doubt to some high-level lunch in Oxford, very different from the tongue-tied outings of the rest of us.

Julian had courage, moral and physical. He was not afraid of being thought cowardly for not tackling low on the rugger field, a practice he thought ineffectual as well as painful. He did not temper his beliefs or behaviour to the accepted codes of boys or masters, and he was prepared to do battle in support of his own. This frequently led to blood and tears because Julian was provocative, uncompromising and combative. He met every attack head on and, while not of Herculean physique, he never resorted to protection from higher authority.

Not only did he not look to the masters to help him out of trouble, but also he scarcely seemed to expect anything of them at all. Unlike most of us, Julian did not regard them with awe. He gave every indication of assuming responsibility for his own education. He read a lot and he liked writing – in a bold hand – but he did not seek to excel in competition with the other boys for the ordinary scholastic prizes. This may have been a reflection of his belief that school was essentially a place of limited and transient importance, a mere frontier stop on the way to adult political life. Not that he regarded Summer Fields, perhaps because he was there, with anything but respect and even affection.

Games, of course, were an extremely important part of school life. In the winter months, Julian, as I have said, valiantly refused to conform to the standards of bravery expected on the rugger field. In the summer I have no mental picture of him playing cricket, or indeed of him out of doors at all except gardening. He had a small plot of land on which he grew cress to supplement the farinaceous school diet. The only game that I recall him playing with any interest was golf. He had a large bag of clubs that would have been very heavy for him to carry for long, yet any danger of this was obviated by a happy self-cancelling process thanks to which there was never any great distance between shots. We were all very much aware when Julian was on the golf-course. The over-size of his golf-bag was matched by the bagginess of his plus-fours which helped to give him a cartoon-like appearance. Not that he intended anything humorous. On the contrary, he took his golf seriously, almost as part of his political persona. After all, had we not seen pictures of Lloyd George and Briand on the golf links?

Julian was not outstanding at work or games, either of which might have won him the respect of other boys; and he lacked that touch of elfin charm and modesty that might have appealed to the masters. He was precocious in his ideas and tastes; he was elaborate in manner; he was sure of himself and none too confident of others; and he was neither self-effacing nor compromising. He was outrageously different. He neither sought nor enjoyed popularity. Yet with his intense courage and his individuality it was possible to see that he would succeed in what he wanted to do with his life, less because Providence had bestowed inordinate gifts upon him than because he perceived at an early age precisely what he wanted to do.

4

STOICS AND EPICUREANS:
NOËL ANNAN AND
ROBERT KEE

I Noël Annan[1]

'I'm going to tell you about something wonderful,' Noël declared in the vibrant tones that came in later years to be his hallmark as a speaker. He was then head boy of Stowe School, addressing us boys of the Lower Fifth. He explained briefly that the master would not be turning up, a surprising piece of information that led us at our desks to snigger and to whisper innuendoes to each other until he seized our full attention by declaring with his arms outstretched and fingers quivering, 'It happened five hundred years ago in Italy. Suddenly people started to paint in a new way.

---

1 Lord Annan, OBE, 1916–2000, Stowe and King's Coll. Cambridge; don and author; m. Gabriele Ullstein; served in WW2, War Office, War Cabinet Office, Military Intelligence; British Control Commission; Fellow and Provost of King's Camb.; Provost of University Coll. London; Vice Chancellor University of London; Chm. Board of Trustees National Gallery; Chm. various committees including one on the *Future of Broadcasting*; Director, Royal Opera House Covent Garden; publications include: *Leslie Stephen*; *Our Age*; *Changing Enemies*; and *The Dons*.

Noël Annan (r.) and Dadie Rylands.

No more beautiful works of art have ever been produced.' He proceeded to talk about the Italian Renaissance with such verve that we were all carried along in a wave of enthusiasm. I don't recall which painters or sculptors he mentioned except for one, Botticelli, every syllable of whose name he enunciated. For the next half hour or so Noël, without a note, prop or slide, held us in thrall; and I am sure that, philistines though we were at the start, we were all by the end awakened for ever to the wonders of the Italian Renaissance.

I was younger than Noël and not in the same league academically, but I was aware that in both personality and achievement he was the outstanding boy of the school. He was both clever and athletic and he applied energy and zest to everything he did. Already knowledgeable about art, he had nothing of the retiring aesthete about him. Nor was he rebellious by nature. His instincts were, and remained, liberal and conventional. At school he was a zealous under-officer in the OTC, and I retain a Ouidaesque image of him marching faster than anyone up and down the North Front at Stowe. He was in the Rugby XV two years running and was always prominent in the pack. At tennis he managed to play for the school, which was more thanks to his determination to get every ball back than to dexterity with the racquet. He shared a study with Nigel Clive, a life-long friend, and when he had half an hour to spare he would listen to classical music on his wind-up gramophone. Music was one of his enduring entertainments. It was always easy for me to imagine Noël singing in grand opera.

Like all boys at Stowe at that time, he owed a great deal to J.F. Roxburgh, the headmaster, who sought to change the ethos of the traditional public school, and to encourage interest in art and architecture. He aimed to know all the boys personally and wished them happy returns on their birthdays. One Sunday he preached a sermon, the main theme of which was the importance of personality. Noël always bubbled over with personality. Immaculately turned out himself, J.F. sought to inculcate a dress-sense in the boys as a manifestation of individuality, and I believe that this has had an enduring influence on many old Stoics from his time. As a general rule they take trouble with their appearance. They can even be called 'dressy'. Their tastes must also have been influenced for life by the beauty of the school's eighteenth-century landscape and temples. In a sabbatical year in the sixties Noël wrote a life of J.F. It was a labour of love, as he himself put it.

Noël's departure from Stowe with an exhibition to King's was accompanied by speculation, among boys and masters, as to whether in later life he would become prime minister or chief of the general staff. When I mentioned this recently to Noël, he dismissed it with a laugh, saying, 'I was not ambitious.' From his mentors at Cambridge, particularly Dadie Rylands, he learnt not to attach too much importance to worldly success; but this did not mean any disparagement of scholastic excellence. On the contrary. This was the Bloomsbury tradition. Noël was formed for life by Cambridge, but, as it turned out, not for politics or the army.

It is surprising that, as an undergraduate in the mid-thirties, an era when many of his contemporaries at Cambridge were deeply engaged in current affairs, some notoriously as communists, Noël had nothing to do with politics. He and his world were interested in personal relations. Several were pacifists. In a portrait of his generation, *Our Age*, published in 1990, he quotes, evidently with approval, E.M. Forster's definition: 'King's stands for personal relations and these still seem to me to be the real things on the surface of the earth.'

He moved much in the acting/homosexual world of the college where Dadie Rylands was his guide, philosopher and friend, his influence more like that of Circe than of Nestor – not, as Noël insisted, that they were ever lovers. He was, as he has written in *The Dons*, 'platonically devoted to him for the rest of his life'. Dadie favoured the rough trade. Noël, like much of Bloomsbury, was intrigued by many aspects of homosexuality. He recalls with delight that, in the nineties, 'earnest' was a code-word for homosexual, as 'gay' is today, and how hugely, on the first night of his most famous play, Oscar Wilde must have enjoyed the irony concealed in the title.

Noël acted once a year in a production of the Marlowe Society and pays tribute to the drilling Dadie Rylands gave there to undergraduate actors and actresses. He taught them that while they were speaking they should learn to think what the Elizabethan and Jacobean blank verses meant, instead of ranting and throwing away the lines. In Noël's view, for three decades after the war Rylands transformed the speaking of verse at Stratford and on the London stage.

Another close friend of Noël from the theatre was Arthur Marshall, who had been a schoolmaster at Oundle before becoming a successful female impersonator. Marshall was also a friend of Rylands, at any rate until he could endure the latter's raillery no longer. Friendship with Rylands, he told Noël, who was clearly all too conscious of Dadies' fickleness, was like being on an ocean liner from which one was hurled into the sea for a misdemeanour, only to find on surfacing a dozen old friends also bobbing in the waves.

Of the main influences from the past that helped to shape Noël's personal philosophy as an undergraduate, one of the most penetrating – and, to me, surprising – was Machiavelli. He recounted in *Our Age* how Machiavelli showed him 'the irreconcilable conflict between the ways of life – the life of personal relations – the inner life ... and the life of politics, of getting and giving, of using power to attain good ends, but ends that are public and not personal'. Another hero was Hume, who taught that our 'passions guide our reason, ... that you cannot prove that men and women have natural rights, any more than you can prove that men will create a just society by following their self-interest'. Like Hume, Noël saw the need to be sceptical and tolerant and to practise detachment. That was why, in the same book, he admits that he 'never believed in the beneficence of collectivism, or of individualism, or theories of rights or utility. But I am not sceptical of the value of reason ... The English politician nearest, perhaps, to my heart ... is Halifax the Trimmer.' He explains how Halifax first favoured Charles II's brother, James, for the throne, but was then foremost in sending for William of Orange when James's policies seemed to be leading to the establishment of a Catholic absolutist monarchy.

Indeed so marked were these influences that some observers have been inclined to see something of all three – Machiavelli, Hume and the Trimmer – in Noël.

You might have expected that Noël's high spirits, and his vitality and eloquence, could easily have been directed to self-aggrandisement. On the contrary, one of his striking characteristics was the contrast between the exuberance of his personality and the modesty of the claims he made about himself. This applies for instance to his work during, and immediately after, the war.

In *Changing Enemies*, an account based on direct experience of the regeneration of Germany, he wrote with Hume-like detachment of the part he played in the analysis of the complicated and often conflicting secret information reaching Whitehall about the enemy's dispositions and intentions. But what required courage as well as intellect was his uphill struggle in the immediate post-war years to try to persuade his compatriots in military government of the change that had come over Germany as a result of the Hitler years and military catastrophe. Germany had repudiated authoritarian government for all time. A new world had come into being there, very different from that of the previous dominant officer-class and the *Beamtentum*. It was not an easy or popular message. In sticking to it Noël made a difference to events, of which the most dramatic incident was his part in the rehabilitation of Konrad Adenauer after he had been sacked by British Military Government as Oberbürgermeister of Cologne.

During the war years in London Noël met Maynard Keynes, a King's man, who was then working in the Treasury. 'I've been reading your reviews in the *New Statesman*,' Keynes said, adding, 'Why not lunch?' This led to regular meetings at the United Universities Club. Keynes persuaded the fellows of King's that with the war ending they must elect some new fellows on spec, i.e. without the customary dissertation. Thanks to this initiative and to Dadie Rylands' support, Noël became a fellow in 1944. A decade later he became provost, after Dadie had turned down the post.

That Noël chose to pursue an academic career rather than one, say, in industry, commerce or politics is some indication of the prevailing *Weltanschauung* of people of his generation, as well as of his own unmercenary and unworldly persuasion. Those who had already been at university before the Second World War tended either to continue their studies or to enter one of the professions. I do not recall a single one of my contemporaries deciding, for instance, to become an apprentice in the manufacturing industry. It was different in France or Germany.

As fellow and provost of King's Noël aimed at bringing about changes that were not revolutionary but necessary if the college was to keep up with the spirit of the times: he persuaded them to pay more attention to research and to increase considerably the percentage of students taken from state schools. His reforms led to a marked improvement in the college's academic standing. He also felt an obligation to assist in the administration of the university, the result of which, he admits, hardly justified the time spent.

Another close friend of Noël at this time was Steven Runciman, a historian of Byzantium and a fellow of Trinity College. They dined regularly once a week, joined by Kit Nicholl, also a Trinity fellow. 'What did you three talk about?' I asked Noël. 'Never,' he answered, 'did we talk about history or the Crusades' (a subject on which Steven was to publish a three-volume magnum opus). 'We gossiped.' Steven, whose father, Walter, had made an unsuccessful attempt in 1938 to solve the problem of Czecho-Slovakia, had a wide range of friends among the aristocracy and royalty of Europe. He was a champion of the unaffected ethos of Cambridge which shunned publicity and whose motto was *nil admirari*, as compared with the showing-off, affected ways of Oxford, as he saw them. Non-political, he was intolerant of silliness in public life.

Gaby, Noël's wife, who had a career of her own as a literary critic and translator, and who did not much favour the prospect of spending the rest of her life in Cambridge, was delighted when they moved to London in the sixties, Noël to become provost of University College and ten years later vice-chancellor of London University. This change also fitted in with Noël's growing involvement in a wide range of activities which included being chairman of a committee on broadcasting, trustee of the British Museum, director of the Royal Opera House, chairman of the National Gallery and president of the London Library – to name but some of the stations of the cross for the great and the good whose pilgrimage Noël had so appositely joined. If he allowed himself such an indulgence, he could take pride in the appointment of Jacob Rothschild to succeed him at the National Gallery, where, in the view of many cognoscenti, he worked wonders.

At the London Library, the members looked forward to Noël's speeches given from the stairs leading up to the gallery running round the reading-room. Their wit, imagery and the animation with which they were delivered were far removed from the usual renderings of the proceedings of a committee.

I am told that the same expectation attended Noël's speeches in the House of Lords after he became a life peer in 1965. In a gathering many of whose members are readier to speak than to listen, Noël invariably received attention and was widely regarded as one of the best performers.

I found it surprising that Harold Wilson, having ennobled Noël, did not give him a post in his government at the time. Many years later I asked Noël about this and he said: 'You know, I would have been no good in a political post. I could never toe a party line completely.'

As in Cambridge, so in London, Noël's time was increasingly taken up with administration – the need, for instance, to bring about the merger of the various medical schools. He learnt the general lesson that British universities will not change their ways except under dire financial necessity. Looking back he was aware of how much time he wasted and how it deprived him of opportunities for thinking and writing. 'The only intellectual', he concluded in *The Dons*, 'is he who evades all responsibilities and executive duties.' But running and trying to improve the university was the task for which he had accepted responsibility, and although he would shy at anything that sounded priggish, it has to be said that Noël could not escape being public-spirited. He recognised that perhaps he mismanaged his time. 'Look at Asa Briggs,' he would soliloquise, 'he's done no less administration than I have, but count, if you can, the number of books he's managed to write.'

Noël had no need to feel deficient in this respect. His first, and perhaps his most original, piece of research led to his essay *The Intellectual Aristocracy*. With feeling he described the leaders of the new intelligentsia in the nineteenth century from whom many later literary and scientific lights are descended. 'There was the sense of dedication, of living with purpose ... also the duty to hold themselves apart from a world given over to vanities which men of integrity rejected because they were content to labour in the vineyard where things of eternal significance grew – in the field of scholarship where results were solid not transient.' He could have been writing about himself, except that, while serious, he was not austere in the manner, say, of a member of the nineteenth-century Evangelical Movement. I would not go so far as to call him a hedonist, but he enjoyed the good things of life and had no guilt about it. Tennis-player, theatre-goer, connoisseur of wine, to the question put to him on *Desert Island Discs* about which luxury he would select to have as a castaway, he replied 'bath essence'. Not the sort of thing a member of the Clapham Sect would have chosen.

He went bald early – very bald – which induced Gaby to liken him affectionately to a seal; and indeed he was a keen swimmer, going to the baths early every morning for lengthy exercise until well into his eighties. His facial expression was invariably animated and his eyes would light up as, with correspondingly lively gestures, he told some story, or, more likely, drew a parallel from literature or mythology. Despite the attention he paid to food and wine he maintained his lithe figure. His movements were as vigorous as his speech. His was always a commanding presence.

His writing conveyed his love of biblical and classical allusions, such as these from different books: 'Like Ezekiel, Churchill breathed life into the dry bones of the JIC'; or 'Nor is it wrong to see Roosevelt, the American Scipio, as the man who gave hope to his countrymen during the Depression', or, describing the impact of a funeral oration by Maurice Bowra, 'the air was so dark with the arrows he despatched, like Apollo spreading the plague among the Grecian host before Troy'. He was a devotee of epigrams, as in this extract from his essay on *The Intellectual Aristocracy*: 'Those who have clear ideas on what life ought to be always have difficulty in reconciling themselves to what it is'; or this comment: 'To move from Oxford to Cambridge is like moving from a gallery displaying the paintings of Veronese and Rubens to one in which are hung the austere simplicities of Piero della Francesca. Cambridge did not pride itself on being the mother of statesmen or an enclave of the metropolis.' In writing in the same book about the evanescence of Roger Fry's fame he averred: 'The recently dead … have a brief life as ghosts, then the grave closes over them. Few return.'

Contrary to what many expected in view of the impact Noël

made on his contemporaries in so many ways, no biography of him has yet been written. The cause lies partly in the very breadth of his interests. In the course of his life he had not concentrated on any single theme or discipline. But I also happen to think that it owes something to his lack of self-promotion and to his indifference to material rewards.

Noël's awareness of how few of his age would mould the future was emphasised by the frequency with which he had to attend memorial services. 'For us the owl of Minerva has folded its wings,' he lamented. Yet for him it provided the opportunity for new flights of eloquence. He became the memorialist of our age. Ann Fleming, Arthur Marshall, Arnold Goodman and Isaiah Berlin were among those friends upon each of whom he delivered an encomium, so poetic that many listening may have felt 'half in love with easeful death'.

His own memorial service was full of surprises, however characteristic. He had made elaborate plans for it, all of which were strictly carried out. It was not described as a memorial service at all, and Noël's name appeared on the front cover of the order of service, but was not mentioned again throughout the proceedings. Epigraphs from Homer, Proust, R.L. Stevenson and Rubén Dario were printed on the cover's fly-leaf. Noël had decreed that there 'should be no grey tinkling on the organ such as precedes normal services', so, as the congregation assembled in King's College Chapel, they heard the organist play, without a tinkle, two Bach fugues and an air from Handel's Water Music. The choir proceeded to the stalls singing words from St Thomas Aquinas. This was followed by some humanistic verses from Cavafy, balanced by two hymns, three prayers and a reading from Samuel, which in turn were matched by three readings from Shakespeare and some lovely singing. But there was no address. Some of his friends regretted this, while others felt it justifiable as nobody could have done it as well as he would have done. I think this omission may have come about simply because Noël, in devising his memorial, characteristically didn't think fit to include an address; whereas, those arranging the service later felt inhibited from tampering with his very carefully worked out plan. Despite this lacuna, I think everyone present felt that the service had been a true and memorable expression of Noël's personality.

Noël had done and written many things. He had 'made a push at chance and sufferance', as he generously judged many others to have done. He made numerous friends. I asked one of them, John Grigg, to say in a word what he regarded as Noël's outstanding characteristic, to which he replied 'enthusiasm'. I agree with that, and I shall never forget the enthusiasm with which he inspired me when I first heard him as a speaker over sixty years ago.

II **Robert Kee**[1]

I'm not sure how I happened to be in Robert's room in the clois-
ters of Magdalen College, Oxford, at the beginning of Michaelmas Term, 1937; but I do know that it proved to be an important
moment for me. Although we had been at Stowe School together,
I had not known him there. From that afternoon when we met
initially as undergraduates in Magdalen, tentatively, and as it were
for the first time, Robert and I became close friends. It was not at
all like the original encounter between Sebastian and Charles in
Brideshead Revisited. Priggishly politically correct though it
sounds, I have to say that neither of us had aristocratic parents, a
fast car, homoerotic tendencies – or a teddy bear.

Only later did I learn that Robert's room had been occupied
by the former Prince of Wales, later King Edward VIII, when he
was an undergraduate. Even if this had been mentioned at the
time I don't think it would have affected our immediate talk,
which, I believe, was about the kind of people, poetry and politics
that we liked and disliked – a conversation conducted in the
none-too-solemn but not totally flippant tones that have run between us ever since.

Not an obviously athletic schoolboy, and with none of the
limb control or co-ordination of his contemporary at Stowe,
Leonard Cheshire, Robert was nevertheless visibly bursting with

---

1 Robert Kee, CBE, b. 1919, Stowe School and Magdalen Coll. Oxford (Exhibr);
author and broadcaster; served WW2, Bomber Command 1940–46, Prisoner of
War; m. (1) Janetta d. of the Rev. G.H. Woolley, VC, (2) Cynthia Judah, (3)
Catherine Trevelyan; BBC *Panorama*; TV correspondent for ITV, ITN
(Yorkshire); Presenter *Ireland* (13 part TV series); and many other TV and radio
broadcasts; his published books include: *A Crowd Is Not Company*; *The Impossible
Shore*; *The Green Flag*; *The Laurel and the Ivy: Parnell and Irish Nationalism*.

Robert Kee, summer 1937.

vitality. He was not so much rebellious as evidently eager to ridicule authority; violent rather than reflective in his reactions. I myself, a boy of theatrical insignificance – and I'm not being falsely modest – caught a glimpse of him stumping into the dining-room at school as if to mark his presence and establish his independence.

Known to everyone for his cleverness, Robert had made a mark at Stowe. A top scholar, he was a protégé of the remarkable history master, Bill McElwee, and of his highly intelligent wife, Patience, both of whom were tolerant of his vertiginous swings of mood and treated him like an adult, discussing everything and everybody, including the other masters, with unexpected frankness. He was also influenced by another exceptional master, T.H.White, the author of *The Once and Future King*, who was then teaching English at the school, and who caught the imagination of the boys by his ownership of an open Bentley and by his dash in the hunting field. Robert learnt much from him about writing.

As with most Stoics, Robert's epicurean instincts were stimulated by the beauty of the buildings, monuments and grounds and by the importance the boys were encouraged to attach to the visual senses. Unsurprisingly, therefore, on arriving at Magdalen, he was captivated by the splendours of its architecture and deer-park. He fitted in quickly there, making most of his friends in college – for instance John Russell, Fred Warner and Bill Cobb.

He was fortunate in his tutors, the first of whom was Bruce McFarlane, a mediaeval historian who demanded the highest standards. After Robert had read him some essay, McFarlane deliberated a moment before saying: 'Listening to you I feel as if a feather-pillow had broken around me.'

His next tutor was A.J.P. Taylor, who stimulated his interest in modern history – as he did mine, though I was not his pupil. Taylor taught him to question all received opinions. The entry of Alan Taylor into Robert's life led to his first emotional crisis – or, rather, embarrassment. Alan's wife, Margaret, fell in love with him. In that age, when a minimal knowledge of French literature was regarded as one of the essential accoutrements of an educated Englishman, some observers liked to see in their relationship a reflection of *Le Rouge et le Noir* even if they could not identify Robert with Jean Sorel. Robert could not respond to Margaret's highly charged feelings, yet, being kind-hearted, and naïve in such matters as we all were in those days, compared to the co-habiting young of the modern generation, he scarcely knew what was going on or how to react. He refrained from a totally dismissive reaction. Besides his humane restraint, his tutor was Alan, which would have made a brutal breach with her awkward. She pursued Robert shamelessly, waiting daily for him to emerge from the library so as to catch a glimpse of him. Subsequently, and more trying for him, when he was serving in Bomber Command she would turn up unannounced at his RAF station. Mercifully for Robert, Margaret before long switched her attentions to Dylan Thomas, with whom she fell in love in no less headlong a fashion.

Remarkably, Robert's friendship and tutorial relationship with Alan did not appear to have suffered from Margaret's fixation on him. Indeed, they remained in touch throughout Alan's two subsequent marriages and until his death in 1990. Robert gave him a party, in which I joined, on his seventieth birthday.

In addition to the trouble Margaret caused Robert at the time, I think that her mad pursuit of him at his highly impressionable age left him with a somewhat derisory attitude to the opposite sex. But this did not last long and any such feelings were well and truly corrected a few years later when he fell in love with Janetta Woolley, whose personality was strong and highly independent.

Handsome, virile, sensitive, witty and possessed of a desire to please, Robert has always been irresistibly attractive to women. His emotional life has been diverse and abundant, but, paradoxically, I don't think you could call him promiscuous; on the contrary, I regard him as uxorious in his own particular way. Not that either in the early days, or at any stage in our friendship, has either of us gone in for confidences about each other's private life. All the same, I like to think that I have played a part in his, having introduced him to two of his three wives.

As a fellow undergraduate, I first experienced the pleasure of Robert's company as a travelling companion, particularly his humour over the disasters or *longueurs* that are inevitable in all lengthy journeys, and certainly were in ours. In the summer vacation of 1939, just before the outbreak of war, he, I and a friend of mine from Hertford, John Vinter, set out on a journey. We had three things in common: innocence, penury and the aim of reaching the shores of the Mediterranean, a destination which Cyril Connolly, our mentor, had taught us must be the target of all travel – something few would think of suggesting today. I had made contact previously with the proprietor of a small hotel on the coast near Toulon who had agreed to feed and put us up in return for domestic help. En route, we spent a night in Paris, which in those days was the Mecca for all students, drawn there by the cheap, bohemian life of the Left Bank. There we drank a lot of wine and underwent, if we did not exactly enjoy, the initiations that the city holds out for the hot-blooded young and curious. At the hotel in the south we carried out, clumsily I am sure, but conscientiously I hope, our allotted housework and managed by the end to have enough money to enable us on the return journey to spend a few nights in Aix-en-Provence.

During our holiday, Robert wore a new pair of royal blue, silk pyjamas. These lent a flash of colour to our simple accommodation, where Robert, with his pent-up energy, his burning eyes and, of course, his pyjamas, had the look of a caged and dazzling animal.

Long afterwards, I proudly took Mary on our honeymoon to stay in the very same hotel in the south of France, which had not changed hands since before the war. To Mary's horror, when we arrived we were shown to a room that was minuscule, had no bathroom and looked straight into someone else's lavatory. Mary took aside the proprietor, whom I had known, and muttered something to him, upon which he said to me: 'Monsieur, vous êtes diplomate.' He immediately ushered us into another much more luxurious room. From subsequent conversation it emerged that he had at first thought that once again I was hoping for free lodging.

Robert joined the RAF in 1940 and became a pilot in Bomber Command. Although aware of the acute dangers to which he was exposed nightly from the effective German air defences, and doubtful of the efficacy of much of the bombing campaign, he nevertheless had no qualms about the cause, and he loved flying. He carried out twenty-three raids over enemy territory before being shot down trying to lay a mine off the Dutch coast. This led to over three years as a prisoner of war, an account of which he published in 1947 in the form of a novel, *A Crowd Is Not Company*. The book was a success. Many years later it was republished as an autobiography under the same title. In a foreword he describes, as follows, the significance to him of this experience as a prisoner: 'I have lived what would conventionally be regarded as a reasonably full life and enjoyed many important human emotions, happy and sad. And yet, re-reading this book, everything that has happened to me since seems somehow secondary to what happened then.'

His liberation from the prison camp by the Red Army is recounted in another book, *The Impossible Shore*, where he describes their brutal if understandable – in view of the *Bundeswehr*'s behaviour in Russia – treatment of the German civilian population. He reveals his gift for metaphor, for instance when mentioning a tiny unpremeditated decision which he took in the chaotic conditions that prevailed after liberation by the Red Army, and which set off a whole chain of independent incidents. This he likened to 'a squib which has jumped into a box of larger fireworks'.

'We could not have lived without books,' he wrote of his prison life, and, to be sure, books have always been essential to Robert. After the war his first wish was to be a writer. For financial reasons he has had to combine this with journalism, written and televised.

A party to which I had been invited by Cyril Connolly, given for Ernest Hemingway in Bedford Square in July 1945, led to an unexpected turning point in Robert's private and working life. I took him along. As a result of the meeting, Connolly gave him an introduction to Tom Hopkinson, the editor of *Picture Post*, where Robert was to work for the next three years. *Picture Post* fitted him perfectly. As he described it later, it was an exercise in photo-journalism, a precursor of TV, based on the conviction that the lives of ordinary people were interesting; that the men who built the *Queen Elizabeth* were those who counted, not the travellers; and that they were to be photographed as if they might have been subjects of Rembrandt. The paper had no overall political stance. I could see that it reflected Robert's ethos at the time.

At the Connolly party Robert also encountered Janetta for the first time. They fell instantaneously for each other, as I knew from the way, almost immediately, I became the odd man out. From Cyril's party the three of us went to dine at the Gargoyle, following which Robert and Janetta disappeared, very much together.

Robert and I lunched with Connolly just before the 1945 general election. We asked him how he was going to vote, to which he replied: 'Apathetic Labour'. This would about have described Robert's attitude. He was never a party man, though interested in politics as a sceptical, liberal-minded observer. He could become engaged and enraged when some major issue arose, as it did over appeasement in the 1938 by-election in Oxford, or at the time of Suez.

He had no wish to be tied down in some institutional framework, which explains why he so quickly left the job in the World Health Organisation in Geneva, where he worked for a short time in the early fifties. I suspect that his reluctance ever to take on conventional, office-bound employment, to become what the Americans call an 'organisation man', which was the response of his nature reinforced by the effects of prison life, may have had something to do with the delay in his being accorded official recognition for his many services to broadcasting and history.

His early thirties proved to be an untidy, unsettled period in his private life. Janetta had left him. He struck up transient relationships with Melinda Maclean in Geneva and Oonagh Oranmore in Ireland, where he lived in some style and where he came under the influence of Irish nationalism. The possibility then occurred that he might re-marry Janetta, but instead he became involved with Cynthia Judah, whom he later married.

But now, in the mid-fifties, Robert suddenly found his voice in public. Special correspondent of the *Observer* in Israel at the time of Suez, and of the *Sunday Times* in Algeria, which was in the throes of a guerrilla war against the French authorities, he then joined the BBC's current affairs programme *Panorama* in 1958. As

Robin Day has said, he was a 'star'. With Richard Dimbleby the anchorman, *Panorama*, a TV magazine, was unique in its early days in the subjects it covered, domestic and foreign, and in the quality of the reporters. They included, in addition to Robin Day and Robert Kee, Michael Charlton, John Freeman, Ludo Kennedy, Jim Mossman, Malcolm Muggeridge and Woodrow Wyatt. Most of them, including of course Robert, had had wartime and journalistic experience. I doubt whether there has since been a current affairs TV team that has had such fire-power. At that time there was no other major TV programme on such matters and *Panorama* became essential viewing for many. People would avoid other arrangements on Monday evenings so as to watch it.

Paul Fox, the editor and producer of *Panorama* and of many other programmes in which Robert participated, has spoken to me of the authority he brought to them and of the courage, moral and physical, that he displayed, for example in Algeria. Another of his TV producers, Geoffrey Cox, has singled out his independence of mind, and his scholarly approach. These, coupled with a dash of Prince Rupert about him, gave his reporting a romantic and compelling quality.

Of course his independence of spirit and his perfectionism sometimes led to rows. His *Panorama* contract with the BBC was abruptly terminated after he wrote to *The Times* complaining of the lack of balance in a programme on the Falklands War. He was not always easy with those he regarded as second-rate. As Charles Wheeler, another of his producers, has put it, he often chafed against the restraints, as he saw them, of the BBC. He was known to cause trouble in the cutting-room. However, speaking of his thirty years with the BBC, ITV, Yorkshire Television and many independent companies, his fellow reporters and his producers are unanimous in their admiration and affection for him.

I think Robert's greatest TV triumph was his BBC thirteen-part series, *Ireland, a Television History*. This was an innovation, making a complicated subject interesting to a wide audience in the UK and Ireland at a time when popular curiosity in both countries about the Irish nationalist cause was in the doldrums. Jeremy Isaacs, the producer of the programme, considers Robert's unique contribution was 'to combine the authority of a historian with the skill of a TV presenter'. The series was based on his book, *The Green Flag: a History of Irish Nationalism*, published in 1972. Roy Foster considers that in this book, as in the TV series, Robert succeeded triumphantly in his aim of producing something that was at once popular and good history. His curiosity and emotions having been aroused at the time, he was strongly critical of the British record, a view he later came to modify.

There's a story arising out of Robert's Irish TV series which casts a sidelight on social relations between the British and the Irish. One day the Duchess of Devonshire, a great friend of Robert's, decided to watch his programme. She was horrified by the revelations of famine, torture and penury. As one of the most brutal passages was appearing on the screen, her butler, Henry, who hailed from Lismore in Ireland where the Devonshires own a castle, entered the room. 'Oh Henry,' she exclaimed, 'I'm so sorry about this. I had no idea.' Upon which Henry said: 'Think nothing of it, Your Grace. Put it right out of your mind.'

Robert's book, *The Laurel and the Ivy: the Story of Charles Stewart Parnell and Irish Nationalism*, published in 1993, continued his mission of bringing home to the British and Irish the reason for the emotional trough that lies between them. His device was to use the enigmatic and romantic personality of Parnell to make human and exciting the nature of Irish nationalism. Again it was an example of Robert's technique of combining narrative skill with scholarship and making it as readable as a thriller.

He has produced novels and many historical studies, drawing often on newspaper reports in a way no other historian has done. He has participated in numerous and varied TV programmes. He has taken up the cudgels on behalf of those who he thinks have suffered from a miscarriage of justice.

In his later years he has found and given happiness in his third marriage, to Kate Trevelyan. He has taken a strong hold of himself to suppress unbridled outbursts such as had scarred his first marriage to Janetta, often leaving her in tears. His character has developed, not just in restraint but in positive consideration for the feelings of others, going beyond mere kindness, as in the generosity of the time and attention he has devoted to Frances Partridge in her eighties and nineties.

Out of the corner of my eye I see Robert as a hero of our time, but essentially a private one, unsung as he would wish. He has been close to his family, despite the occasional lapse; a charming and, dare I say, a flattering companion, apt to look on the bad side of things to avoid complacency; an enjoyer of life without being indulgent; and, above all, a friend, ready, as when I first glanced shyly at him over sixty years ago, to talk both enthusiastically and disparagingly about books, writers and people we have known.

5

EARLY DAYS WITH FRANK

'I can't remember how you castle,' Frank Longford[1] whispered to me across the chessboard. 'I think we'd better stop playing,' I whispered back, glancing at the crowd that had been gathering around us. We quickly restored the chess pieces to their original position, and left the table. In doing so Frank, who always likes to salvage something from a seemingly humiliating situation, managed to drop rather loudly the name of his uncle, Lord Dunsany, mentioning in an aside that he had been an excellent chess-player.

We were attending the annual Hastings Chess Tournament in the 1950s and had become bored watching the two grand masters at play in the centre of the room, so decided to have a game ourselves on one of the boards set out on the many surrounding

---

1 The Earl of Longford, KG, b. 1905, don, politician, author, philanthropist; m. Elizabeth Harman, lecturer and student in politics, Christ Church Oxford; personal assistant to Sir William Beveridge, Minister of Civil Aviation; First Lord of the Admiralty; Lord Privy Seal; Secretary of State for the Colonies; Leader of the House of Lords; Chm. the National Bank; joint founder New Horizon Youth Centre. His publications include over 30 books.

Frank Pakenham when Minister of Civil Aviation.

empty tables. We had not been playing for long before some of the crowd watching the grand masters moved away from them and started to follow our match. Hence Frank's whispered SOS to me and our hurried exit from the scene.

I recall another time with Frank in Sussex, again many years ago. I was recuperating by myself on the south coast after an illness abroad. Frank telephoned. Bernhurst (his home) was snowed up. Could he come down and join me for the day? I was delighted and met him at Brighton station. He was carrying several daily papers, the *New Statesman*, *Tribune*, Sir Theodore Gregory's Stamp Memorial Lecture on central banking, a book on the fiscal system and a life of Christ. 'I wonder if I could have a cup of coffee?' he asked as I greeted him on the platform. I drove him to the pier where at the far end we found somewhere that announced 'Morning Coffee'. It was a desultory place, but Frank didn't seem to mind. Aware of general atmosphere, he is nevertheless insensitive to the details of his surroundings. What matters is to be able to talk and this he did with the same continuity as the rolling of the waves beneath us. It was a mixed flow: Evan Durbin, George Martelli, Oliver Franks, Anthony Eden and the difficulty of being a socialist banker.

After our coffee break we took a walk on the cliffs outside Brighton and then drove along the coast to Rottingdean, where Frank was eager to see the house in which Kipling had lived. It displayed a commemorative plaque. Peremptorily, Frank rang the doorbell. Nobody answered. I guided him to the Kipling Museum housed in the fine eighteenth century house opposite, called The Grange. Frank is not a natural museum-man but he was taken with the library below the museum. On one of the shelves he found a copy of his autobiography, *Born To Believe*, and looked to see how often it had been taken out. He was gratified by the results, the more so when he compared them with the parallel figures for the other biographies on the same shelf. He became immersed in a copy of Napoleon's memoirs and proceeded to read passages aloud, to the evident astonishment of the several elderly ladies demurely choosing a novel for their daily read. Unperturbed, Frank extracted from the shelf a biography of Field Marshal Alexander, from which he read to this captive library audience a paragraph about a speech that he, Frank, had made when the field marshal had first spoken in the House of Lords.

It was time for lunch. It was time to give the library a break. So I dragged Frank away rather reluctantly. As he left he said in a loud voice to the librarian: 'Very nice library you've got here.' She looked a little baffled.

When we arrived at English's fish restaurant in Brighton we found it full. The proprietor was unresponsive when I asked for a table; likewise when, at Frank's prompting, I enquired whether we could cash a cheque. They didn't cash cheques for strangers. Then Frank said: 'It's Lord Pakenham.' The climate changed immediately. We were offered a table and were told that it would be quite all right about the cheque. A waiter took our coats, promising to brush Frank's, which was covered with mud from a fall he had had during our morning walk. He produced a menu and asked: 'Are you alone?' Frank hesitated a moment and I could sense that he was ruminating something. Then he said: 'Yes, but fortunately my friend doesn't know it.' Not surprisingly, the import of Frank's piece of theatrical dialogue was quite lost on the waiter.

At lunch Frank talked uninterruptedly, as he always likes to do at mealtimes. Lady Dorothy Lygon has described how, as a young man at a weekend party, he would take a hearty helping of smoked haddock at breakfast and show utter disregard for the bones. 'They interfered', in her words, 'with neither his conversation nor his mastication, both of which continued unimpeded.'

The same insouciance about what he was eating appeared when Frank was visiting a friend at her home one evening. She took great trouble with the *décor* of her house and liked to fill the many small tables in her sitting-room with bibelots. It so happened that this evening when Frank was there he was sitting next to a console covered with shells of varied shapes and colours. No sooner was he seated than he stretched out his arm, grabbed a handful of shells and started eating them. His conversation flowed as always but it was accompanied by the crunching of his hostess's treasured shells. In the early days of our marriage Frank used to visit us and he would never leave the house without taking an apple from a plate on the dining-room table and munching it as he said good-bye.

To return to the south-coast outing with Frank in the fifties, after lunch we went for coffee to the Royal Albion Hotel. This was to satisfy Frank's wish to experience vicariously some of the vice that he imagined had gone on there in more profligate times under Preston's hotel management before the war. 'I believe', Frank confided to me as we entered the hotel, 'that Preston used to go up to people when they arrived, as it might be you and me now, and offer them a glass of champagne.'

I asked Frank what he wanted to do during the afternoon. He said he wished to explore the Bloomsbury country that lay around. He had been reading about Virginia Woolf. She had lived at Rodmell, near Lewes. The Bells and Maynard Keynes had lived at Firle. 'Couldn't we go and look over their back gates? We might get an impression.' That then was our itinerary. We set off in the car, Frank talking all the while, his mind apparently inexhaustible. We had had quite a bit to drink at lunch and I know that I was beginning to feel drowsy. But Frank continued, touching on his time at the Admiralty when he had been First Lord. He had found it necessary sometimes to slip out between meetings of the Lords of the Admiralty to consult a psychiatrist. 'My trouble was', Frank explained, 'that, as I confessed to the doctor, I hated the sea. The psychiatrist explained my difficulty this way: "You are having difficulty in your relations with people and water represents the medium separating you from them."' In describing this consultation, Frank, who was seated beside me in the car, began making undulating movements with his hands, saying that it was with similar gestures that the doctor had indicated the relevance of the sea to his problem. Then suddenly in the middle of this gripping story he fell asleep. For him there was no transition between wakefulness and slumber. Sleep happened instantaneously.

A few days later Frank invited me to lunch in the House of Lords. The other guests were Lord Attlee, who was to take his seat there that afternoon, and Lord Lucan, a descendant of the hero of the Charge of the Light Brigade, who was then a Labour whip in the Lords. Though unexpectedly apprehensive about the initiatory proceedings he was about to undergo, Attlee was sprightly. He told us he had been reading Magnus's *Life of Gladstone* and had been astonished to learn that the GOM had managed at times to avoid calling a Cabinet meeting for as long as three months on end. With a wry smile he recounted how he had evolved a way of getting through Cabinet meetings with minimum delay. He had always begun by praising the paper under discussion, saying to the minister responsible that he presumed he did not wish to add anything to so admirable a presentation of the case. That usually silenced him. Then, instead of asking everyone if they agreed with the paper, an invitation that would surely have led to many expressions of doubt about this or that detail, he would say: 'Well, if no one has any objection, we'll let that go.'

Regardless of chronology, I have to record here, because it shows Frank's ready wit, an exchange between him and Harold Wilson that took place in the Cabinet in the sixties. At some meeting Frank asked if he could go to Ireland to take part in the celebrations of the Dublin uprising. The Prime Minister said no, arguing in support of his decision that some members might equally ask to go to Vietnam to celebrate their cause. Frank retaliated by saying in deadpan fashion that he did not know of many members of the Cabinet who had family homes in Vietnam.

Continuing my diversion from the calendar, I should explain that I first got to know Frank well during the early years of the war. We were both unfit for military service and were working in London. We were both ashamed at not being in uniform and this served as a bond between us. Frank helped to assuage his guilt by writing an article about it that was published in *Horizon* under the pseudonym Neuro. As was his way, he did nothing to conceal his humiliation. Robert Kee, a close friend whom I had introduced to Frank, told me of a typical encounter with him when he, Robert, was serving in the RAF and was stationed near Oxford. He had gone to dinner there with the Pakenhams, who were eager to hear every detail of his experiences flying bombers over Germany. After Robert had given a graphic description of how difficult it was to see the targets and how effective was the German anti-aircraft fire, Frank, visibly moved and humbled, implored Robert to try to arrange for him to be allowed to take part in one of their bomber missions. Robert became equally moved by Frank's attitude.

Frank and I shared lodgings in London in the immediate post-war years before and after my time in the British Embassies in

Washington and Athens. I was not married and Frank's family were living in Oxford. We stayed, first, in the painter Constable's studio in Charlotte Street, at the back of a house belonging to Mary Hutchinson. Her world was that of Bloomsbury and there was a marked incongruity between her talk of Matisse and T.S. Eliot and the subject that preoccupied Frank at the time, his relationship with Attlee, in whose government he was serving. Letters from Attlee in reply to those from Frank threatening resignation used to lie about. They were written in Attlee's laconic style and were invariably limited to saying that he had received Frank's letter, the contents of which had been noted. Mary Hutchinson was intrigued by Frank's eccentricity, while Frank, many of whose relations were artists or writers, some of whom tended to regard him as a philistine, was pleased to think that he had a foot in their world.

On my return from abroad in the early fifties Frank and I shared a flat in Sussex Place. We had a dinner-party there at which Mary, to whom I was then engaged, provided the food and the guests were Mary Hutchinson and Donald Maclean, an old friend from Washington, then serving as head of the North American Department in the FCO. It was at the height of the Korean War, about which we had an argument over dinner, Donald revealing marked sympathy for North Korea and antipathy to the USA. He became drunk and was aggressive to us both, particularly to Frank. The evening was a disaster, except that it provided me with an important alibi a little later when Donald and Guy Burgess had disappeared behind the Iron Curtain and the Security Service was looking for a third man who might have tipped them off that they were about to be arrested. I took the initiative in revealing to them that I had been involved in a row with Donald at a dinner, which would hardly have occurred had I been in cahoots with him. I was also, incidentally, able to disclose to the Security Service something they had not then come across, the existence of an official minute of mine concerning the Korean War about which Donald had complained, saying that I had no justification for writing the way I had.

After we were married and had moved into a small house, Mary was a little surprised by the impression Frank gave that, as he saw it, nothing much had changed, except that she had joined the party, in which she could now do the odd spot of cooking and housekeeping. It is one of the contradictions of Frank's character that, in many ways unconventional to the point of being regarded by some as a traitor to his class, and pro-Irish in sentiment, he nevertheless has the traditional English attitude of his generation to foreigners, believing that non-whites start at Calais. He had some difficulty in coming to terms with the fact that Mary was Greek, as became embarrassingly apparent when he spoke at our wedding reception and told of his surprise, when he first met her, at the paleness of her complexion.

I was delighted to go on seeing Frank as much as ever, and this only came to an end when, in 1953, I was posted to Vienna. Meanwhile, we had begun seeing his wife Elizabeth on her visits to London. She was aware of, and resigned to, Frank's eccentricities. It was no good trying to change him. He had always been like that from the day of their marriage – an event about which she was happy to regale us. Dressed in cream satin with love-knots and carrying orange blossom, roses and lilies of the valley, Elizabeth arrived at St Margaret's, Westminster for the wedding, but there was no sign of the bridegroom or the best man, Freddie Birkenhead. She waited. She continued to wait. Eventually they turned up, having gone by mistake to Westminster Abbey. They had been surprised to find the dearth of congregation there, but Freddie said consolingly to Frank: 'People don't go much to weddings nowadays.'

Before Elizabeth became a prolific mother and writer, she was a most promising politician. 'The Madonna of the Barricades' was what she was called from her appearance on the hustings in 1945. But, as Frank has written, she gave up the idea of a political career in the interests of him and the children. Hers has been a remarkable career, not least in her relationship with Frank. When they were staying with us once, and were on the point of going to bed, Elizabeth told us that every night at home Frank asked her: 'What time are they going to call us?' and every night she answered: 'Who's they?'

This flippant picture I have given of Frank should not lead anyone to overlook his serious purposes in life and his achievements. He believes in success and, as his daughter Judith has recorded, he is always drawing up lists of the ten best of everything. He has also been on a life-long crusade, even if the location of the Holy Grail has frequently shifted. Elizabeth expressed it to me once thus: 'He has always had a burning sense of mission about something or other.' The cause has usually been unfashionable or downright unpopular; he has always been on the side of the underdog. He has been heroic in the face of much derision.

But to return to my earliest times with Frank, over half a century ago, clear in my memory is a piece of worldly wisdom that he then gave me. Growing up, he told me, was a process of discarding the incompatible elements in one's character. Yet, as I now realise looking back, in nobody I have known have the elements been so mixed as in him. No one has harboured within himself so many contradictory qualities and impulses as he does: piety and worldliness; intelligence and naïveté; humour and messianic fervour; a striving for humility and a passion for publicity; pride in ancestry and belief in equality, approving, for instance, the role played by the hereditary peers in the House of Lords while accepting their elimination. No one could have pursued, with such enthusiasm, so many contrasted causes – Ireland, Catholicism, the reconstruction of Germany, world government, the care of prisoners and the mentally handicapped, penal reform and the suppression of pornography – nor enjoyed so varied a career. He has been don, politician, banker, publisher and author (over thirty books on subjects ranging from the peace treaty with Ireland to President Nixon); he is the father of a large, distinguished and varied family; and he has displayed, at any rate to me, a unique talent for friendship.

6

A DOUBLE-FIRST MEETING

Jack Kennedy[1] and other members of his family were the guests of the British Ambassador in Washington. They were playing 'The Game', a form of charades. It was the first occasion on which I met the future President of the USA, then a young congressman. It was also the start of my time with my first ambassador, Archibald Clark Kerr[2], then recently ennobled as Lord Inverchapel – a name that the Americans invariably pronounced with the stress not on the first syllable as it should have been, as, for instance, in Inverness, but on the second, as in invertebrate.

It was March 1947, the month when President Truman announced the Truman Doctrine, in which Washington took over the UK's commitments to Greece and Turkey, and pledged US support for democracy and 'free peoples' everywhere. The Doctrine was a landmark in post-war US foreign policy. Looking back

---

1 John Fitzgerald Kennedy, 1917–1963, President of the USA 1961–63.
2 Archibald Clark Kerr, Baron Inverchapel, GCMG, 1882–1951, m. Maria Teresa Diaz Salas; Minister to Chile and Sweden; Ambassador to Iraq, China, the USSR and the USA.

*Archie
Inverchapel,
British
Ambassador,
Washington.*

to that stage in my life, I am aware of the strain of earnestness within me that was apt to obtrude and that made me wonder then at the incongruity between the merriment of the party in the Embassy and the gravity of events in the world outside. It was as if we were acting out parts in a game of consequences. But neither Jack, nor his elder sister, Kick, the widow of Lord Hartington, nor Eunice, another sister, much admired by Hugh Fraser, who was also a guest at the party and at that time an aspiring young British politician, seemed to find it at all odd that they should be being entertained at this time, in this way, in the British Embassy.

It has to be said that, perhaps as a frivolous reaction to former austerity, a craze for round games and quizzes gripped much of the immediate post-war social world of Washington. This could be embarrassing, which was half the point. For instance, a regular entertainment at the annual New Year party of a respected Washington cave-dweller was to ask the guests to write down who they thought would be dead by the time of the next year's party. The previous year's prognostications were then read out. One evening when I was present this game proved to be a veritable exercise in gallows humour since several of those forecast as dead were sitting around hale and hearty, if not happy, at the party.

Having just arrived at the Embassy, I watched with fascination and some surprise how Lord Inverchapel disported himself that evening with the Kennedys. I knew something of his reputation. 'Archie?' his colleagues in the Diplomatic Service would say, 'Well, of course, we all know Archie', by which they meant that he was unconventional, and full of contradictions, being for instance both a bit left-wing and on friendly terms with the Queen, but likeable and, it had to be said, successful. The Queen to whom I refer was Elizabeth Bowes-Lyon, whom Archie had known when they were both young. I once asked her, many years later, what her recollection was of Archie. 'Oh,' she said, 'Archie was different', which struck me as an aptly succinct description. He had been ambassador to China and the Soviet Union before his appointment to Washington. In the eyes of his colleagues he wasn't exactly bogus, a favourite term of description in those days, but there was a touch of make-believe about him, even if he was down to earth in appearance and character. He was totally lacking in the pomposity that was then apt to cloak people occupying important public positions. To paraphrase the kind of charm that

Lloyd George was said to exercise, no bird would have been safe on its perch within range of Archie.

Pipe-smoking, tweedy, with rugged good looks as though he spent much time out of doors, and a broken nose, the result, he was proud to recall, of early boxing, he made much of his Scottish ancestry and had even changed his name to give it a more Gaelic ring, an enhancement well-known throughout the Service. In later entries in *Who's Who* he described himself, not as a diplomat, but as a farmer; in earlier entries he gave his birthday as five years later than it really was, and when this was found out he omitted any date of birth at all. He also made no mention of his birthplace – Australia – and gave no school, recording merely that he had been 'educated privately', whereas in fact he had been a student at Bath College. According to his biographer, Donald Gillies, both these last two omissions should be attributed, not to snobbery on Archie's part, but to his sensibility to the snobbishness of others!

He was eager not to appear out of touch with modern writers; the works of Auden and Spender lay about in his study. He took pains in drafting and wrote with a quill pen. He knew nothing of economics, which made him seem as incongruous in the post-war world as it rendered him sympathetic to his contemporaries in the Service. His ethos was more that of Harold Nicolson than of Gladwyn Jebb. He did his best to counter the appearance of old age. The foreign secretary, Ernest Bevin, on a visit to Moscow when Archie was ambassador there, had been so impressed by the vigorous way he walked about the Embassy stripped to the waist, and by the evident respect that he had earned from the Soviet leaders, not to mention by his inimitable charm and reputed radicalism, that he chose him to succeed Lord Halifax at the Washington Embassy. He arrived there accompanied by a footman, who was in Archie's own words 'a Russian slave given me by Stalin'. This gift raised many eyebrows in Washington where McCarthyism was just getting into its stride. By some Archie was regarded as soft on communism. Rebecca West told me years later that she was sure Archie had been a Soviet agent. By many he was thought flippant in the way he answered serious questions. He disliked the staid atmosphere of Washington social life and did not click with the leading hostesses, Mrs Beale and Mrs Bliss, who were taken aback by his compulsive urge to shock and to tell risqué stories – a reflection partly of his shyness.

He was married twice – to the same person, a small, neat, pretty Chilean whom he appeared to treat as if she were a delicate *objet de vertu* that should be kept on the chimney-piece. Archie preferred male company. Above all, he adored the young.

Not surprisingly, therefore, he was greatly enjoying the party with the youthful Kennedys. They threw themselves into The Game with the characteristic family verve, though the way Jack moved suggested some slight physical inhibition. We all knew of his suffering in the war. He appeared to be more taken with the company of his family than with anyone else; and they likewise. They were all theatrically informal, lounging and haring about in the palatial rooms of Lutyens' residence and bursting with nicknames and family jokes. So far as I could judge, they showed little interest in the decorative splendour of the Embassy, which no doubt they took for granted, having lived themselves in luxurious surroundings. They struck an introspective young onlooker from the Old World as exceptionally extrovert. If any of them held sway over the others it appeared to be Kick, who, without being at all *grande dame*, was possessed at once of the family vitality and a quiet authority. From a casual glance, Jack mercifully did not, so far as I could detect, bear any outward traces of his notorious father, who had made such an unfortunate impact on the London scene during his pre-war time at the US Embassy there.

I had rather expected Jack, who had spent some of his formative early years in the London Embassy, to take the opportunity that evening to ask how things were faring in the old country. But not at all. This may have been because he was entirely absorbed in The Game, like the others – in trying to convey by mime the personality of Eleanor Roosevelt or the physiognomy of Neville Chamberlain. However, I felt then, as I did on observing him later, that the subject did not interest him closely. Not that he was at all *blasé*. He seized on any fact floating around that intrigued him. But as with most of his compatriots, his imagination continued to be fascinated by Winston Churchill and was scarcely fired by Clement Attlee.

He could not fail, of course, to show his innate charm. He was totally without pomp. It was the first time that I heard the Kennedy accent that was later to ring unforgettably round the world. He was dressed casually, in American style. Everything about him seemed to me, who had so recently arrived from England, to be very American, not least his macho reaction when, for instance, the name of some Englishman cropped up. 'Yer know,' he said with disgust, 'that guy wears a sweater with buttons all the way up.' Contemptuously, he drew his hand up and down his chest.

His looks were extremely attractive and youthful; indeed there was something boyish about him as he flashed his broad smile upon one – his magnetism was animal-like and unself-conscious, though he was aware of it and laughed, as if to say 'I know'. If, in the mood of charades, you had had that evening to choose a canine equivalent of Jack you would not have thought of either a terrier or a sheep-dog: he neither barked aggressively nor shook benignly. Perhaps an English setter would have done. There was no doubt from his repartee on this occasion that, added to his other qualities, he had an extremely prompt wit – not the self-serving, somewhat elaborate humour often to be found in public life but a quiver of verbal arrows that were self-deprecatory and rapid in their delivery, qualities in him that alone had something British about them. While on that subject, it has to be said that, unlike one or two British politicians of the time, he did not seem to depend on alcohol for the necessary social stimulus.

Alas, the evening offered no chance to observe the trait in Kennedy's character, later so significant, of an irresistible interest in the opposite sex. Not surprisingly, it doesn't seem to have occurred to Archie to invite any unattached glamorous girls. But, as already suggested, Kennedy appeared, at any rate on that occasion, to find plenty of entertainment in the company of his sisters.

It cannot, of course, be claimed, on the basis of Jack's company during just one evening of seriously frivolous entertainment at the very outset of his career, that it was possible to say whether or not he clearly possessed the essential presidential timber. But to any observer of this brief occasion, there can have been no doubt of his unique and attractive personality, of a certain inner magic about him despite the very openness of his manner, and of his close involvement in his large, dynamic and devoted family.

7

OZYMANDIAS AT OXFORD

I was in my cell-like office in the Chancery in Washington one afternoon soon after Sir Oliver Franks[1] had arrived as British Ambassador. There was a gentle knock on the door and Franks put his head round to ask tentatively, 'May I come in a moment?' I stood up in some confusion, wondering what on earth had prompted this unheralded visit. Franks came in, sat down in the chair by my desk, stretched out his long legs and, puffing at his pipe, asked me, with a slight inclination of the head, 'How's your father?'

At that time my father was Drummond Professor of Political Economy at Oxford. I muttered something about his health, which had not been good, to which Franks responded sympa-

1 Lord Franks, OM, GCMG, KCB, KCVO, 1905–1992, don, government administrator, ambassador, banker and chairman of many important committees; described by his biographer, Alex Danchev, as 'one of the founding fathers ... of the post-war world'. Provost of The Queen's Coll. Oxford and of Worcester Coll. Oxford; Lord Warden of the Stannaries and Deputy Chairman of the Prince of Wales's Council; wartime service in the Ministry of Supply; Ambassador to Washington, 1948–52.

*Oliver Franks at
Nantucket.*

thetically before taking another puff at his pipe and moving into higher gear: 'One has to remember the difference between genesis and result.' I have to say that my thoughts were on a distinctly lower level than this, if they were thoughts at all, rather than daydreams. I had just had lunch. I was looking forward to a game of tennis later in the afternoon. Nevertheless, I hope I appeared sufficiently alert and eager to learn. In any case, Franks continued: 'An idea thought up for one reason and to meet a particular need may have completely different consequences.' He went on to explain how, contrary to expectations and intentions, the economic planning staff of the Treasury had come into being under Stafford Cripps; and, more pertinently, how a speech by Ernest Bevin about Western European Union could well be leading to negotiations that would end in something much more far-reaching than originally expected, which, to descend to brass tacks, meant the impending negotiations that were to lead to the North Atlantic Treaty.

Franks came to make quite a habit of strolling down the corridor of the Chancery for an afternoon chat. He told me quite early on in a matter-of-fact way that he found it relaxing. It was essential to set aside periods of rest. He planned his day accordingly. I couldn't help contrasting it in my mind's eye with Friday afternoons with Ernest Bevin when I was in his private office and he would relax after a hard week's work by serving Harvey's Bristol Cream sherry, which he poured out with plenty of follow-through, and let his mind 'expand', as he called it, which in fact resulted in him telling stories.

Bevin's name often cropped up in Franks's relaxing sessions because they had had many dealings together during the war when Bevin had been Minister of Labour and Franks a senior official in the Ministry of Supply. Bevin had been responsible for Franks's appointment as chairman of the Marshall Plan negotiations and then as ambassador in Washington. No better example could be found of the harmony of opposites. Franks believed that Bevin had the power of right judgement, which Socrates considered to be the highest virtue. In his biography of Oliver Franks, Alex Danchev has said of his subject that if he ever 'stooped to sin, it was to take a quiet pride in his own power of right judgement'.

One day, some time before the 1948 presidential election in which every mortal being and every poll knew that Governor Dewey was going to win, Franks was leaving my room after one of his afternoon relaxations. He caught sight of a headline in an evening newspaper: PRICE OF BUTTER DROPS. With his head tilted forward he said: 'Significant. It may be helpful to Truman.' It probably was; at any rate Truman won the election contrary to all predictions. Franks was an early apostle of the 'it's the economy, stupid' school.

In a more than usually reflective mood Franks said on one occasion: 'We in the industrial West are not going to find it easy in the future. We are teaching the rest of the world how to manufacture things and they will soon be able to do it as well as we can.' I don't at all remember my response but I expect, as in a university tutorial, that it was to repeat more or less what Franks had said, as if to be sure that I had got it right. There was a pause. Franks was almost as much a master of the pause in conversation as later I was to find Harold Pinter to be in drama. Franks took another pull at his pipe. More silence. I noticed in his visage a slight wrinkle of the lip, an Ozymandian trait, that contrasted with his otherwise impassive features. Switching the subject, he said almost explosively: 'You know, what the world needs nowadays is more poets.'

I can't say that these afternoon sessions were as relaxing for me as Franks found them for himself. But they enabled me to get to know him and to be able to express his thoughts more easily on paper. This became important when the negotiations for the drawing up of what eventually became the North Atlantic Treaty began in earnest. Franks played a key part in the talks which were held with the representatives of the other potential treaty powers as well as senior officials of the State Department. In innumerable meetings he managed, by raising doubts, asking questions and making very gentle suggestions, to lift the discussions from a series of statements of national viewpoints to a plane where all were endeavouring to reconcile minor disparities for the achievement of an aim of great importance to them all. After these meetings I would return to the Embassy with Franks and he would leave it to me to draft a telegram that reflected his thoughts on the outcome.

Naturally, I was much reassured by this mark of confidence. I was astonished by how seldom he drafted anything himself. He wrote very little throughout his long and busy life. He left behind no diaries or personal papers. In retrospect I have found this odd in someone with such a career and such an academic cast of mind. When I discussed it with Isaiah Berlin, he said that one of Franks's strengths was to know what he could and what he could not do. He knew that he didn't have an exceptional literary talent. Franks was just about himself, as, like Aristides, he was just about everything. So where, I asked Isaiah, did he think Franks's special qualities lay? To which Isaiah replied: 'In exerting his intellect. He gets things right; he is sure-footed. There is no intuition or hunch, just intense mental activity.' Isaiah went on to recount an occasion when Franks got it wrong. This was when Franks invited him to work on the Marshall Plan. 'I felt', Isaiah said, 'that I was being summoned by God. I could not refuse, though I knew it was a mistake. When the prophet Jonah was summoned by God, he refused. I did not do so. Everybody realised in a day or two that I was hopeless.'

Lord Roll, who knew Franks well in the Marshall Plan days, said that he had always been 'mindful of political realities'. I was struck immediately when I started to serve him in Washington by his realism, his political awareness, and his focus on the end-result – not qualities I had expected to find foremost in someone from the academic world who was so uncynical and seemingly so detached.

Married to a Quaker and brought up in a strict nonconformist background, not given to back-slapping, shy by nature and thinking before he spoke, he was not someone who was tailor-made for success in the USA. Yet Franks knew where and how to win esteem, which was by being his unself-seeking, high-minded and liberal self in circles, of which there are many in America, that respect such qualities. Very tall, always calm and unshowy in manner, he had a distinctive but unobtrusive presence. He managed to establish close and valuable friendships, of which the most important was with Dean Acheson, the Secretary of State. Acheson later described how this relationship had come about: 'On an experimental basis I suggested that we talk regularly and in complete confidence about any international problems that we saw arising.' Accordingly they would meet for a drink in the evening. No publicity was ever given to this. It lasted until Franks left Washington, and whatever advantages it may have brought Acheson there can be no doubt that it was of inestimable benefit to the British Ambassador – who came to be better informed on US foreign policy than his staff, which was unusual and could be as gratifying for him as it could be awkward for them.

After Washington, Franks was offered all manner of prestigious posts – editor of *The Times*, governor of the Bank of England, secretary-general of NATO – but he turned them all down in favour of becoming chairman of Lloyd's Bank, and then provost of Worcester College, Oxford. He became the panjandrum of important enquiries, including one into the financing of Oxford colleges, whose report included the magisterial rebuke to

All Souls: 'When we reviewed the record … we were compelled to infer infirmity of purpose.' He chaired the commission of enquiry into the origins of the Falklands War which, to the indignation of Lord Callaghan, exonerated the Government from all blame for not having foreseen or forestalled it.

His Grove of Academe was Oxford, where he was a successful philosophy teacher and college head, but it would be fair to say that he did not stamp his personality on a generation at the university as did, for example, Maurice Bowra. What is unique about him is that he applied an academic bent of mind not to Academe, but to the worlds of government, diplomacy, banking and public enquiry.

It was in the context of a very different, and it might be thought incongruous, role that he had held, that I was to have my last meeting with Franks. I had just taken over from him as vice-chairman of the Prince of Wales's Council in the Duchy of Cornwall, to which was attached the Gilbert and Sullivan-sounding title of Lord Warden of the Stannaries. The estate of the Duchy of Cornwall included the Scilly Isles, where Franks owned a house. One of the attractions of the place for him, so it was said, was the opportunity for fishing, or, to be more precise, for shrimping. Harold Wilson also had a house there, not, it has to be said, that they sought out each other's company, let alone went shrimping together in the tidal waters of the Atlantic.

So far as my appointment to the post of Lord Warden was concerned, it was to prove a disastrous example of central miscasting. Before I succeeded Franks, I was a member of the Prince of Wales's Council and was able to observe the masterly way in which he contributed to the affairs of the Duchy. A question arose, say, of whether the Duchy should go to the expense of installing some new pig-sties on one of their properties. The secretary of the Duchy would make a presentation, following which the members of the Council would express their views. When Franks was asked for his advice, which often happened, he would pause an instant before giving a most lucid analysis of the pros and cons of different courses of action. He seemed to me to apply just the same clear powers of reasoning, just the same calm objectivity, to the problem of the building of the pig-sties in Cornwall as he had done in my presence some forty years previously to the structure of the North Atlantic Treaty. The outcome too was similar because, after this exposition, there didn't really seem to be any problem at all. The answer was self-evident. The only question was why on earth the rest of us had taken so long to see it.

After I took over from Franks in the Duchy, I was to prove quite incapable of filling the role as he had done. To the identical sort of issues that continued to arise I failed to do justice to my lofty position. I gave peremptory answers; I did not appear to be able, or at any rate to be ready to apply to them the same degree of ratiocination as he had done. There was a hiatus in the workings of the Council. They felt short-changed. My opinions came to be decreasingly sought. One day it was suggested at the highest level that I should go to see Franks to obtain his advice on how I could conduct myself as he had done. This I proceeded to do as quickly as possible.

I motored down to Oxford and rang the doorbell of Franks's large house in the northern part of the town. He answered it himself and welcomed me with an offer of tea. He disappeared and emerged some time later bearing a tray laden with cups etc.

Clearly there was no servant in the house. He had recently had two hip replacements but, characteristically, he didn't complain. He was getting on with life as best he could. He poured out the tea and I posed my dilemma. Could he help me to become more like he had been in the Duchy? Without showing any surprise or emotion Franks applied himself to this question with predictable matter-of-factness. To begin with, it was necessary to understand the characters with whom one was dealing. While calculation had to be applied to decide upon the appropriate course of action, the heart was part of the equation and could not be left out of account. He proceeded with the necessary analysis. I listened as if to a tutorial. I left fully briefed.

But although, when I returned to the Duchy, I tried to apply the lessons I had learnt from the maestro in North Oxford, I did not succeed and before long it was felt that someone else would be more appropriate than me in the Duchy. I had to agree. How could I ever have thought that I could emulate Franks?

The proximity of Shelley's tomb in the High at Oxford to Queen's, a college directly opposite, where Oliver Franks was at one time provost, may have contributed to the tendency of his contemporaries to liken him to Ozymandias. There was something in the comparison, as I realised, both at my first meeting with him in Washington in 1948 and at this, my last, in Oxford. Certainly, he had a look of cold command but, as I had got to know him in earlier days, I perceived his sensitivity to human failings and his interest less in his own life than in that of others.

The question that sprung to mind on first, as on last, acquaintance was why someone so modest, so reserved, and so eager to shun the limelight, a philosophy teacher whose spiritual home was Oxford, should have become such a worldly success. How had he managed to persuade ministers, officials, diplomats, dons, or members of committees of enquiry, regardless of nationality, to see things as he did? Without egotism, with no wish to dominate or steal the limelight, confident in himself while aware of his limitations, he was imbued with a sense of public service. But his secret lay first in the reasoning power he possessed of divining where truth – the right course – was to be found, then in the exercise of great restraint to avoid disclosing too categorically his own conviction, and finally in his ability to raise doubts, to ask questions and to make tentative suggestions, so that really there could only be one way through the maze. That I believe was the explanation of why Oliver Franks became, in British public life, the most influential man of his age who never held elected office.

8

ROY JENKINS AND HIS WORLD

Every coterie needs a playground. The playground of Roy Jenkins[1] and his world at the time when I first remember them was the tennis court in Ladbroke Square. The entourage included at this early stage the Gaitskells, the Ian Gilmours, the Mark Bonham Carters, the Jo Grimonds, Douglas Jay, Tony Crosland and Ann Fleming. Ali Forbes may have fitted into a category of honorary or out-of-country members. One or two others, including Woodrow Wyatt, Bill Rodgers, Shirley Williams and a few from Roy's ministerial stratosphere, notably John Harris, David Dowler and Hayden Phillips, revolved later in close orbit. Obvi-

---

1 Lord Jenkins of Hillhead, OM, b. 1920, Chancellor of Oxford University; former leader of the Social and Liberal Democratic peers, and of the Social Democratic Party; s. of Arthur Jenkins MP; m. Jennifer Morris (created Dame); served WW2 in RA; Labour MP, 1948–76, MP for Glasgow Hillhead, SDP/Alliance 1982, SDP, 1982–87; former Minister of Aviation, Home Secretary, Chancellor of the Exchequer; Deputy Leader of the Labour Party and President European Commission; Honorary Doctor of 17 universities; publisher of 22 books, including major biographies of Dilke, Asquith and Gladstone.

*Roy Jenkins
playing tennis.*

ously, Roy also had many political colleagues who did not feature prominently in his leisure time in those early years.

Mary and I first entered this cosmos in the late 1950s or early 1960s when I was working in London between posts abroad; and although I continued to keep up with the members it never seemed quite the same in later years, perhaps because I was living abroad most of the time, but also because many of them had achieved high office or fame and had become busier – and more competitive. At any rate I find myself recalling vividly this early stage of Roy's world.

Tennis in the Ladbroke Square garden on Sunday afternoons was one of the most honoured rituals of the group. This, of course, was before Roy had acquired a country house at East Hendred. Tennis was his favourite game, except for croquet, in which he displayed more confident mastery.

I could never quite make out why Roy was so keen on tennis. If one part of his game could be singled out as even less good than the rest it was his serve. It was an elaborate performance that started with him walking back to the rear enclosure of the court, then turning round and advancing fast and purposefully to the service line where he would stop abruptly, swing his left arm fiercely, and, with an audible intake of breath, give the ball an almighty blow – the result of which, whether in pace or direction, rarely did justice to the careful preparation and windmill activity that had gone into it.

The grass courts in the square afforded just that element of surprise and hazard that Roy loved. The unpredictability of the surface and its chalk lines also appealed to Douglas Jay, or at any rate favoured the particular qualities of his game, particularly his method of scoring. He was a regular Ladbroke Square player, and, being a Wykehamist, he played to win, but to do so unobtrusively. This was not at all the impression given by Tony Crosland, who was often his partner. He was theatrically languid and liked to play with a cigarette hanging casually from his mouth. He dressed quite elegantly but distinctly down for the occasion, so that if the rest of us were wearing white he would be dressed in grey – just as later in official life when others wore a prescribed white tie and tails he would turn up in a dinner jacket. With it all, Tony on the tennis court displayed much charm, which was not directed at anyone in particular, and he laughed a great deal, often in the middle of rallies.

Playing against these two, Roy and I came to realise that many points had to be won twice over. This was so especially following those strokes we thought our best. First, we had to get the ball over the net and then, if it was a deep shot to the far baseline, we had to shout 'in' before there was any chance of Douglas giving his contrary verdict upon it. Tony feigned not to mind whether it was in or out.

Roy liked this aspect of the struggle. He also relished the chance for back-chat and quips that tennis provided. We were competing one Sunday afternoon against Douglas and Tony. It was soon after the 1959 general election, which Labour had been expected to win. Gaitskell had been convinced of victory. Defeat had immediately been followed by acrimonious inner-party strife over Clause 4. In the game of doubles that Sunday, Roy and I had started well. We were just on the point of winning when we started to lose badly. Roy was about to deliver one of his inimitable serves when he checked his customary delivery and said: 'It's just like the Labour Party; we seem to be snatching defeat out of the jaws of victory.'

Apart from his interest in the game itself and the complicated task of winning, Roy was, I believe, sensitive, as always, to his surroundings. On those late afternoons, he liked the sunlight flickering through the trees and the row of houses in the square seen intermittently through the branches. Architecture is one of his realms of acute observation.

The Jenkinses lived in the square and we went to their house for tea after the tennis. Tony may well have looked forward more to the tea than to the tennis. Despite their rivalry, Tony clearly liked chatting to Roy. He professed to despise social life, regarding it as degrading and a waste of time. He used to criticise Hugh Gaitskell for going out so much. Dora Gaitskell told me that she had once said to Tony: 'You shouldn't be so intolerant of people who like company. It's merely that your tastes are different. You just like sex.' She didn't tell me how Tony had replied.

Jennifer Jenkins was a keen tennis player, better than Roy, and she enjoyed the game partly because she thought it good for Roy to take exercise – this was before he took to jogging. But she disliked Tony's habit of inviting himself in for meals and then staying on afterwards and telling the Jenkinses how much he had disliked the other guests. 'He used to go on about it,' Jennifer exploded, recalling his effrontery, 'as if he thought he had some mission in life to stop us seeing our friends. In the end I told him not to come any more.' I could imagine the angry way she must have spoken. Jennifer can get quite cross, so that, as Ann Fleming put it, 'an attractive flush comes over her cheeks'. Jennifer would often conclude discussion of Tony's behaviour by saying: 'Of course, Tony's always been very jealous of Roy.'

'However,' Jennifer said later over tea on one of our tennis afternoons, 'Tony doesn't want to come round so much now. He's decided that we won't be in opposition much longer and therefore he's got to use all the time available now for reading. He's drawn up an enormous list of all the books he must get through before the election. He says he's going to devote himself to it ten hours a day.' Jennifer thought this immoderation typical. Roy would never have thought of spending a whole day like that. Early on in life he formed the habit of waking early and devoting an hour or two to reading something other than official papers – hence the systematic and successful stocking of his mind with

English literature and biography. Soon after he became Home Secretary he told me that he had started to read Proust through once again from beginning to end.

Another form of exercise at this stage was football, which took place on Saturday afternoons with the Gilmours at Ferry House in Isleworth. The youthful dexterity of the Gilmour boys was literally overwhelmed by the grown-ups, men and women, who threw themselves boisterously into the game. Mark Bonham Carter was a keen forward, Roy an equally keen, if less mobile, half-back, Caroline Gilmour was fast on the wing and Bernard Levin was invariably consigned to goal. Karl Miller, who had recently abandoned a career in the Treasury for literary journalism, took an invitation to play football one afternoon at Ferry House rather too seriously. He turned up wearing studded football boots and a striped shirt. The 'little lot', as Caroline liked to dub the world in which Roy moved for his recreation, was aghast. Here was an amateur trying to be a professional, whereas it was their philosophy to be professional while giving the impression of light-hearted amateurism.

Roy has said that he found Tony the most exciting friend of his life. The competition between them for office, starting in Wilson's first administration, didn't affect Roy's feelings for him, however much it may have dislocated the regular tramlines of their relationship. He admits in retrospect to a sense of unease at having voted for Edward Short rather than Tony to succeed him as deputy leader of the Labour Party. He has always made a cult of friendship, devoting to it more than a routine MOT-type schedule of maintenance; so that, while not being able to suppress the strong instinct of rivalry, he keeps up the struggle, almost in defiance of nature, to prevent it interfering with friendship. Unlike most ministers, Roy in his friendships does not draw a distinction between politicians and officials. He does not keep the latter at a respectful distance. At the Home Office, the Treasury and the European Commission in Brussels the members of his private office were central to his life at work and play.

Entertainment has been an essential component of Roy's friendship, whether in his private or official life. He hates lunching or dining alone. Even when he became Home Secretary and had several boxes of official papers to read overnight, he avoided, if humanly possible, anything in the nature of a quiet evening at home. He even preferred to attend some police dinner than have to endure that – as his private secretary has told me, though he may not have put it quite like that to the policemen. What he likes, as he has put it himself, is 'general social life but not endless political gossip in a narrow field.'

First at Ladbroke Square and then at East Hendred, Jennifer and he have regularly given lunch and dinner parties for a wide-ranging list of guests. Nowadays at East Hendred, which Dick Crossman described as 'a rather ramshackle old vicarage', it is only lunch parties that are held. Seated at the head of a smallish rectangular table, Roy dispenses claret, drawing details of the château and the vintage of the wine to the attention of the guests, whose eyes may be tempted to stray to the array of empty double-magnums of *grand cru* that stand on the sideboard as memorabilia of previous, but of course not grander, occasions; while Jennifer, at the other end, has the considerable task of carving and serving the food.

Labour leaders seem to have difficulty in adjusting to Roy's life-style, which they obviously expect to be more grandiose than it is. On top of Crossman's disparaging description of the house, Barbara Castle, after being a guest, wrote critically of the lunch there. She had expected *cordon bleu* cooking, only to be disappointed at being served meat and two veg. Roy was delighted by this reflection on Jennifer's fare. She doesn't pamper him, knowing that he makes up elsewhere for any simplicity in the diet at home.

Roy's eating and drinking proclivities are a matter of fascination to his friends. How does he manage it, they ask. He minds a great deal about where and what he eats and could be considered a devotee of Cyril Connolly's dictum: 'Treat every meal as your last'. In the published diary of his time as president of the European Commission, he records with Wisden-like detail the duration and menu of many of the dinners and banquets given in his honour in different parts of the world. He confesses to having been made ratty by the poor service on a flight between Brussels and London, and by the incompetence of an Irish waiter in opening a bottle of wine – 'an unusual Irish deficiency'. He complained to me recently that his literary output had been seriously impaired when his doctor had put him on the water-wagon for a couple of weeks.

The elaborate detail he has garnered from *Who Was Who* and from electoral records has increasingly characterised his writing. Such personal researches have proudly demonstrated, for instance, that he was 'the only person ever to have sat in Parliament for the three biggest cities – London, Birmingham and Glasgow – of post-industrial Britain'. Or, enquiring into the backgrounds of the chancellors of the exchequer about whom he was writing, he discovered that 'ten of them were Oxbridgians, five from each,

only three … were Etonians … only two had serious landed property … two began their lives in humble circumstances … and six
at the very modest end of the middle class … none was a crook,
or even a full cad'. He has worked out that a swing of fifteen votes
would have made him rather than Callaghan Prime Minister after
Wilson decided to leave Number 10.

His friends have come to be very much aware that Roy's passion for the minutiae of everyday life applies to his interest in the
weather and in the passage of time, this last causing him to take
frequent glances at his watch. 'I have always been too weather-in-
fluenced,' he admits. This was unfortunate, but inevitable, in
Brussels. Writing of a spell there in June 1977, he moans: 'There
have been seventeen consecutive days in which the sun never
once appeared.' He comments that, when the results of the election for Chancellor of Oxford University were awaited, 'the sun
did not waste itself upon this *dies non*.' Of his timetable as Chancellor, he says that it 'involves a good quarter of my time and energy, but as it has come to provide something more like a half of
my interest, the balance is a favourable one'.

It wouldn't be quite right to describe him as calculating; his ef-
fervescent humour is for ever on the alert to observe how readily
things go wrong, but he hates wasting time and in temperament
he's not happy-go-lucky, nor bohemian.

As Roy approached his seventies his companions observed
how he managed to pursue with undiminished vigour three careers: politics, writing and the chancellorship of Oxford University, each of which was quite demanding in itself. None seemed to
conflict with the others. On the contrary, they may have been
mutually helpful.

How far, for instance, has his literary reputation been of assistance to him in his political career? Oddly, I have never heard Roy discuss this openly, though he has no inhibition about analysing in public his official life. I have a shred or two of evidence on this myself. I happened to be in the party that accompanied Harold Wilson to Washington on his first visit to the USA after he became Prime Minister in 1964, and on the outward journey I observed that he read Roy's life of Asquith (which incidentally Roy regards as the book by which he would most like to be judged). When he put it down I heard him say something to the effect that anyone who could write that was fit to occupy a prominent place in British politics. Without indulging in *post-hoc*ery, one is tempted to point out that Roy was made Home Secretary the following year.

Over a decade later, when I was Ambassador in Paris, I had a few words with the President of France, Valéry Giscard d'Estaing, about Roy's candidacy to become President of the European Commission. He wanted to know more about him. I told him of Roy's reputation as an author, and, at his request, I gave him the titles of some of his books. The President left me with the impression that he would have a look at them, and I heard later that he had been much impressed. Of course, it does not follow that this was the reason why he supported Roy for the post, but, given his interest in literature, it is fair to say that it may have helped.

The influence Roy has undoubtedly exercised over Tony Blair has owed a lot to the historical perspective in which he sees and describes the current political situation. The forces in the country that inspired the great reforms of the beginning of the last century were split by the emergence of the Labour Party alongside the Liberals. In pointing this out in interviews and articles he underlines the importance of understanding the past in order to make the right decisions about the future.

Turning the question the other way round and asking how far his political experience may have helped Roy as a historian, it may be pertinent to invoke Gibbon's well-known reflection in his autobiography: 'The captain of the Hampshire Grenadiers has not been useless to the historian of the Roman empire.' It is arguable that Roy's manoeuvres on the battleground of Westminster may have been even more instructive to the writer than those of Gibbon on the military parade grounds of the southern counties. Roy's first steps in biography, his short life of Clement Attlee, coincided with the start of his political career and his association with politicians; and his early and direct understanding as an MP of the workings of Parliament was a springboard for his book about the reform of the House of Lords, *Mr Balfour's Poodle*. In fact politics and politicians have provided the setting and *dramatis personae* for his whole *oeuvre*. Direct experience has also been the impulse for many a maxim from him such as that David Owen's nuclear fetishism was in accordance with 'the rule that most politicians and all political parties cannot leave internally divisive subjects alone'.

His literary output has been prodigious. This is not the place to review his work but I have to draw attention to one unique feature of it because it also colours his conversation and the way he looks at people and events – his use of metaphor and simile. He describes Wilson's style of leadership in circus terms as 'more like that of the acrobat skilfully riding a bicycle on the tightrope than of the ringmaster imperiously cracking the whip'. Heath, in the

1975 referendum campaign, revealed a certain awkwardness in his character, without wishing to be awkward. 'He stood resolutely there, as impervious to the waves and as reliable in his beam as a great lighthouse, but sometimes blocking the way.' Of the effect on this country of President Giscard's close collaboration with Chancellor Helmut Schmidt, he observed it 'spreading downwards like water seeping from the surface to the root of the plant', thereby institutionalising the Franco-German partnership and leading the two to 'reconcile their differences bilaterally and *pas devant les petits pays*' (in which Britain was included). According to Roy, Denis Healey 'has long carried light ideological baggage on a heavy gun carriage'.

He has said that he could not have devoted his whole life to writing, and this does not surprise me since, when I first knew him when we were undergraduates at Oxford just before the war, there was no doubt of his intention to apply himself to public service in some form. Roosevelt and Keynes were his heroes. They still may be. He went into politics, while always seeing current events in historical terms, and writing extensively about them.

I cannot comment here at any length on Roy's political career, about which he has been frank and revealing. He likes to speculate on whether he would have become Prime Minister had he devoted himself more wholeheartedly to party politics. I don't know about this but I do know that, as he himself admits, if he had pursued this course it would have been against his nature. I have heard him say that he would have enjoyed being Prime Minister more in retrospect than at the time – a remark perhaps more of a historian than of a totally dedicated politician.

Of his time at the Treasury he reflects, with characteristic imagery, that economic management 'by its very nature leaves only footprints in the sand. The tide of the next chancellor washes them away.' He is proud of his reforms at the Home Office in the 1960s. His overall conclusion about his political career is that it has given him more influence on events than he could have had in any other walk of life. Certainly, when he was President of the European Commission, his influence was decisive in the creation of the European Monetary System, a landmark on the route to closer union. For forty years he has been the most forceful and influential British advocate of more wholehearted UK involvement in the creation of such a union, second only to Edward Heath.

An incident occurred during Roy's time in Brussels that illustrates some of the many sides of his character. He had made a speech critical of the Soviet Union over their invasion of Afghanistan and about the penalties in trade that might ensue. The French Ambassador complained to him afterwards that Paris would deeply disapprove if the European Union were going to ban the sale of butter to the Soviet Union. Roy admits that his reaction was fairly offhand. He was fed up with the way the Ambassador always treated Paris as the Areopagus of Europe. Ill-temperedly and dismissively he simply said: '*Quel dommage.*' Roy's temper was not improved by the discussion at the subsequent lunch, when other ambassadors to the Community also expressed concern about butter. He protested that, faced with Afghanistan, they seemed unable to raise their gaze above the milk churn. Afterwards, through the mediation of the French Ambassador's wife, he did his best to make it up with the Ambassador, admitting that it was partly his fault, not on the grounds of substance, but through his having shown a lack of courtesy.

I think that this event shows Roy's propensity to blow up in discussion if aggravated beyond a certain point, his talent for invective when roused, and his eagerness, while holding his ground, to avoid causing residual feelings of personal resentment.

I consider that not the least remarkable feature of Roy's public career has been the influence he has continued to exercise, despite the passage of time, on those, much younger than himself, who have become prominent in public life. He may not have broken the mould of British politics in the way he wanted but, through his writings, speeches and personal contacts, he has secured widespread support for his conviction that a realignment of parties and electoral reform are needed. They are essential if the will of the many who belong to the non-ideological centre is to be represented in Parliament.

In the conclusion of his autobiography, Roy remarks that he has a lot of friends and a lot of interests. He might have added that he remains a great enjoyer, never curtailing pleasure to accord with some supposed political correctness. Tennis, alas, is out, but not croquet or conversation or claret or travel. To all who hope they still belong to his world and know him as a friend, his zest for the good things of life does not seem to be in any way incompatible with other equally prominent traits in him, evident from the early days I have described – his passion for writing and his intense, courageous and creative commitment to the public causes in which he believes.

9

THE FOUR GEORGES

'Hurry up now ... Last orders.' The publican's voice rose above the clinking of glasses, the boisterous laughter and the general hubbub round the bar of The Boot, our neighbouring pub, to be answered by predictable calls of 'Same again' and 'Make it a double', when suddenly a shout was heard above the clatter: 'Mr Ten to speak to Lord Jellicoe[1],' followed by 'Phone over here.'

George made his way to the telephone which was behind the bar. Mary and I moved closer and were able to hear him say in a tone of extreme sobriety against the conversely bibulous accompaniment of the revellers: 'There's nothing I would like more.' And again: 'There's nothing I would like more.'

When he rejoined us he confided that Edward Heath, who was

---

1 The Earl Jellicoe, KBE, DSO, MC, PC, b. 1918, son of Admiral of the Fleet 1st Earl Jellicoe, m. (1) Patricia O'Kane (m. diss. 1966), (2) Philippa Dunne; served WW2 Coldstream Guards, SAS and SBS Regiments; Foreign Service in Washington, Brussels and Baghdad; Minister of State, Home Office; First Lord of the Admiralty; Lord Privy Seal and Minister, Civil Service Department; Leader, House of Lords; chairman and director of many companies; Chancellor Southampton University; President Royal Geographical Society.

George Jellicoe with Archbishop Damaskinos, 1944.

in the process of forming his government after his general election victory two days earlier, had telephoned to ask him to become Minister in charge of the Civil Service, as well as Leader of the Government in the House of Lords. 'It's all right now,' George said, 'but it might not have been had things gone differently.' I ordered a bottle of champagne to celebrate, and we heard about the possible snag that had been surmounted.

Apparently, some time previously, George, at the end of an exhilarating evening, had been stopped by the police. He was charged with driving beyond the legal alcohol limit. Luckily, the case had been put off until after polling day, and the press had maintained silence about it, as would have been unthinkable had it occurred a generation later. Nevertheless, there was cause in George's mind for anxiety, as had been apparent when he had been watching the election results with us on the night of the poll. The story might break, and Heath, who had reacted calmly when George told him about it, might have second thoughts. George had kept on insisting to us defensively that it was far from certain that he was about to enter the Cabinet. However, he did, and when the case came up and he was found guilty the damaging consequences of being deprived of his licence were happily offset by the acquisition of an official car and driver to which he was entitled as a minister.

George is a man of moods. He is not a complicated but a many-sided character. There are in fact four Georges: there is George the First, the unabstemious, boisterous Lothario, with a leer like a roué in a Peter Arno cartoon, blessed with an iron constitution and athletic prowess that enabled him to have been on the verge of the British Olympic ski and sleigh teams; then we have Hero George, the dashing man of action, a leader who, whether descending by parachute or commanding by sea, kept the enemy on tenterhooks in the Eastern Mediterranean throughout the war; thirdly, there is George the aesthete and sightseer, who, with little finger raised, will speak discerningly of paintings, mosaics and furniture, a great patron of the arts, his talent as a collector *manqué* only due to lack of funds, which has not prevented some bold purchases; and finally we have pensive George, scholar and public servant, concerned to promote the national interest, high-minded, cautious and conscientious.

George also has had four careers – as soldier, diplomat, politician and businessman – but it cannot be said that any one of them has paired off exactly with any of the four sides of his character.

A striking and irrepressible feature of that character has been his easy communion with members of the opposite sex, and this may have been prefigured by an early experience. He spent some time as a small boy in New Zealand where his father was Governor General. George wanted to become a wolf cub, but no pack was available, so instead he joined the Brownies. He got on very well with them.

Having four older sisters and being the only son, George received plenty of attention as a child. He still does in the circle of his family and friends, helped by his joviality and his loud and jocular bantering of Philippa across the dinner-table.

George's ebullient personality did not develop early; certainly not at Winchester, of which school, incidentally, he is a most untypical representative, being neither reticent nor undemonstrative. It was Cambridge that brought him out. An exhibitioner at Trinity College, where Steven Runciman was his tutor, he got a First in Part I of the History Tripos. He made many friends there, the three closest of whom were killed in the war. He skied, played golf and absorbed some practical knowledge of claret. He had by now acquired the physique of the proverbial ox.

The war was the *Glanzpunkt* of George's career. It was glorious. He served with the Commandos in the Middle East where, on sick leave after being wounded in the Western Desert, he ran into David Stirling in the bar of Shepheards Hotel. Stirling was looking – and where better to look than there – for a second in command of the Strategic Air Services (the SAS). George, who then served under him, greatly admired his powers of leadership. Stirling was captured in 1943, after which the SAS was split and George was given command of the Special Boat Squadron (SBS). Ian Patterson, who was in his squadron, said to Mary later: 'We'd follow him anywhere; if he told us to walk across the sea, we would.'

With four Free Frenchmen, George landed in Crete from a Greek submarine and succeeded in blowing up more than twenty German bombers on Heraklion airfield. The next call to action came just after the Italian Armistice in 1943. True to form, George was dining in the main hotel in Beirut. Summoned urgently to Cairo, he was told there to proceed immediately to Rhodes to persuade the Italian commander-in-chief of Italian forces in the Aegean to join the Allies. George scoffed at the means of transport offered to him and chose instead to land by parachute. He was fired upon by Italian soldiers and, as he was under the strictest orders not to let his instructions fall into enemy hands, he decided to tear them up and eat them, which proved to be difficult as they were printed on embossed paper. Eventually, after shouting 'amici' many times, he was led to Admiral Campioni's headquarters.

Despite his forensic skills, deployed in prolonged negotiation, he did not succeed in his mission. The Germans had strong forces on the island and, as George later admitted, it would have been impossible for Admiral Campioni to have taken them on.

Within days George took his SBS squadron to a series of islands in the eastern Mediterranean where he persuaded the Italians to rally to his side. But the Germans soon recaptured the islands and George was taken prisoner. He quickly escaped and was able, in his last campaign of the war, to take part in the liberation of Greece. In October 1944 he led a mixed force to the Peloponnese to hasten the Germans' withdrawal. From there he proceeded to Athens to establish a British presence before the communist-controlled guerrillas in Greece (ELAS) could do so. He arrived there, not by parachute but on a bicycle. Mary, who had been in Greece during the German occupation, witnessed him entering the Grande Bretagne Hotel just after the Germans had relinquished it. He quickly reappeared on the balcony and was greeted by a huge crowd below shouting 'Yellicoe, Yellicoe'. Mary recalls how struck she was by seeing him there and by how even more struck she was by seeing, alongside him and his fellow officers, the buxom figure of Sophie, the girl who had 'served' the commander of the SS camp where she, Mary, had earlier been imprisoned. Sophie seemed quite at ease with her new masters, and they with her.

The next day Mary accepted George's invitation to go with him as his interpreter to Thebes for the liberation of the town from the Germans. George insisted that she should sit in the front of the jeep as she was the heroine of the hour. This proved to be a double-edged compliment since she soon became the target for the tributes of vegetables and sticky grapes thrown by the peasants lining the roads, while George sat inviolate high up at the back.

George joined the Foreign Service soon after the war and it was not long before he showed his mettle. He was attending the Council of Foreign Ministers meeting in Moscow in early 1947 as a very junior member of the British delegation. Some of the

British team had been delayed and George found himself the British representative on the highly important committee dealing with the future frontiers of Germany. He received a note from Ernest Bevin, the British Foreign Minister: 'Sorry to have landed you with this. Let me know if you need any help.' George replied: 'Thank you, Secretary of State, I'm OK. If you need any help I shall be glad to oblige.' Bevin was delighted.

I served alongside George in the Chancery of the Embassy in Washington, his first diplomatic post abroad. He was an amenable and life-enhancing colleague. He was as conscientious as anyone could be in the Chancery by day, as he was as rumbustious as it was possible to be in Washington by night – which did not amount to very much. His recreation was mostly tennis. He and I often played as doubles partners on the Embassy tennis court against Donald Maclean and Denis Allen, the head of Chancery.

George's next posting was to the Embassy in Brussels, where he was much impressed by Paul Henri Spaak's constant pleas to Britain to commit itself wholeheartedly to Europe. His term in Belgium made an impact on his attitude to Britain's relations with the European continent which has remained constant afterwards, however much the politically correct view in the Tory party has changed on the subject.

He was then transferred back to London for a spell in the Northern Department of the Foreign and Commonwealth Office, a post which I later held, and which we both found was one of the most rewarding in the career.

From London he was sent to Baghdad to serve as the deputy secretary general of the Baghdad pact. This enabled him to indulge his passion for travel. I have been on several journeys with him, the last to Sicily when we were both over eighty, and he is the most inveterate traveller I know, a tireless sightseer, scouring and remembering the detail of guidebooks – happy as the day is long provided it can end with red wine and Armagnac. In the Middle East he became addicted – to use his own word – to the marvels of the Iranian landscape. These he visited with Philippa, who was living with him in Baghdad following the breakdown of his first marriage. The FCO were shocked by George's illicit affair. Sir Derick Hoyer Millar, the Permanent Under-Secretary, said that he must either give up Philippa or leave the Foreign Service. George has told me that he never had an easier decision to make. He had liked and benefited from his time in the Service but he did not feel bound body and soul to it for life, as he did to Philippa. So he resigned.

He had to find another career. George is not by nature a political animal. He has never been a wholly committed party man. For a time just after the war he sat on the Labour benches in the House of Lords; and he made his first speech there after the war from the cross-benches. He is imbued with public spirit and is instinctively drawn to the public service. I regard him as a casualty of the eclipse of Empire. He would have made a most convincing governor of Bengal or Viceroy of India.

Some time after he resigned from the FCO one or two Tories got in touch with him and this led to him accepting the appointment of Lord-in-Waiting in the Lords. I attended a small dinner party early in 1961 to celebrate – we always seemed to be celebrating with George – his first step on the political ladder. Much predictable wit was exchanged about the waiting the Queen would have to do. In 1963, after two junior ministerial appointments, he was made First Lord of the Admiralty.

He didn't like being in Opposition where he found himself from 1964–70 – the years of the Wilson Government – but he was busy as front bench spokesman, dealing, *inter alia*, with foreign and defence affairs. He also actively promoted ideas for the reform of the House of Lords. Then, as already recorded, the chance came to join Heath's Cabinet in 1970. In his role as Minister for the Civil Service he secured the indexing of the pensions of public servants, for which he should have won their undying gratitude.

When he was a minister, whatever the demands of his social life, George would get up very early in the morning and 'do' the boxes thoroughly. Clever at mastering them, he was always well briefed. He got on well with his officials and won the affection and respect of his fellow peers, who regarded his far from dogmatic, not to say somewhat hesitant, manner of speech as a sign of integrity. To the question I once put to Peter Carrington about what particular quality George had brought to the handling of business in the House of Lords, he answered without hesitation, 'personality'. I think that the same could be said of his contribution to his other careers.

Alas, 1973 proved to be the pinnacle of his political career. He was forced to resign over a scandal that was not really a scandal at all but a case of mistaken identity leading to a miscarriage of justice. This is what happened. Lord Lambton, who held a junior ministerial office at the time, was involved in some public charge of impropriety in the course of which the authorities gained possession of the engagement book of a certain notorious prostitute

in which the name Jellicoe appeared. Fearing that this would become public knowledge in the course of the Lambton enquiry,
Edward Heath, who was then Prime Minister, sent for George and
asked him to give an account of any extra-marital relations in
which he had been involved. George confessed that he had indeed
had relations of this kind and agreed to resign so as to avoid the
public outcry which the authorities seemed to fear would occur if
he did not do so. In fact, as it emerged later, the name Jellicoe in
the incriminating engagement book had had nothing to do with
George. It was the name of a block of apartments in Maida Vale
where the prostitute plied her trade. George had never been
among her customers.

Although, at the time, George was upset at this blow and the
hoo-ha that had been aroused, I think he soon came to see it as an
act of serendipity, a stroke of luck. It paved the way for him to
enter upon another career rather than having to serve a further
spell in political opposition, which he would otherwise have had
to do. On the other hand his friends have resented very much the
unfair circumstances that brought about his downfall and the
way his name is apt to be dragged in whenever the press mentions
Lord Lambton or reports upon some case of immorality in high
places.

His subsequent business career as director and chairman of
large companies, including Tate and Lyle, and Davy Corporation,
had many attractions for him. It meant constant, and often distant, travel, thereby responding to his deep-seated *Wanderlust*. He
told me once of the pleasure he always found in sinking into a
seat on a jumbo jet and waiting for the take-off to no matter
where – and for the promised refreshment. It also brought him

into contact with the developing world, in which he has always been interested.

According to his senior colleagues at Tate and Lyle, the company was going downhill when George took over. His arrival was a turning point. With his personality, energy and contacts he gave the company a new structure. Such was his impact that Tate and Lyle is now the biggest sweetening company in the world. An ironical fact about this – though it should not be whispered abroad – is that George cannot himself stand the stuff.

George's lack of pomposity never left him even when he was engaged upon the most serious business. His conviviality and informality invariably helped to make things go, however much they may sometimes have caused surprise. In the course of his many public speeches he developed on occasion a somewhat ponderous manner of delivery, and the listener could be excused for not knowing whether this was to underline the seriousness of the point he was making or to herald the arrival of a joke. Leading a high-level British trade delegation to Tokyo, he was called upon at the end of dinner to say a few words of thanks to his Japanese hosts. 'In speaking to you at this important juncture,' he began rather heavily, 'I have to tell you that I am a much diminished man compared with the person I was when I sat down at this dinner.' A pause followed. Translations were whispered. The Japanese smiled. George continued: 'Yes, I took my shoes off at the beginning of the evening, and now I can't find them.' There was a longer pause and further translations. The Japanese smiled even more. They had heard tell of British humour.

From what I have been told, George has had a heartening influence on the many companies and institutions in which he has held a prominent position. Although a man of action, and eschewing the writing of anything himself, he has given rumbustious attention to his multifarious, non-political, non-commercial posts, *inter alia* as chairman of the Medical Research Council, chairman of the Council of King's College, London, chancellor of Southampton University and president of the Royal Geographical Society. I have to mention these responsibilities, however briefly, because they illustrate the importance of the academic/aesthetic side of George's character.

To give a final glimpse, I have to show George with Philippa at Tidcombe, his home in Wiltshire. He is looking out of the window at the distant downs, and, closer at hand, at the garden for which, as he has done frequently over the years, he has just purchased a large quantity of shrubs and bulbs. Philippa, whom he invariably and correctly describes as 'my long-suffering wife', has once again been delegated the task of finding space for them all and of having to undertake the major work of planting everything before the onset of winter. George is immensely happy with the scene.

10

ANN FLEMING
IN HER ELEMENT

'Roy Jenkins is the author of a number of books including *Mr Balfour's Poodle*,' announced the chairman of the Swindon Labour Party, introducing Roy at a meeting of the Party just before the 1970 general election.

At this announcement Ann Fleming[1], who was sitting next to me, whispered, 'That'll please all the dog-lovers.' I laughed. She went on, *sotto voce*, 'They think it's a book about dogs like Joy Adamson on the lioness.' There was indeed a round of applause which Roy acknowledged with a wide beam. I was struck, as must have been the citizens of Swindon, by how fit he looked, as if, despite the election campaign, he had spent the last weeks on holiday in the Mediterranean. By contrast the others on the platform looked distinctly pale.

The chairman went on to declare that Roy, who was then Chancellor of the Exchequer, was the architect of the Labour

---

1 Ann Charteris, 1913–81, m. (1) Lord O'Neill, (2) Viscount Rothermere, (3) Ian Fleming. The comment was made about Ann's marriages: 'Something seems to go wrong in the taxis from the Registry Office.'

Ann Fleming at Sevenhampton.

Government's economic recovery. He read out, proudly but unfluently, as though describing the traits of some strange animal at a circus for the first time, the main features of Roy's career.

My daughter Alexandra, Ann Fleming and I were attending a meeting of the local Labour Party in the Swindon Town Hall. Alexandra and I had decided to go from a mixture of curiosity and solidarity, Ann from an expectation of fun and mischief. She had for some time occupied an official position in the Swindon Conservative Party. When she heard about the meeting and that I was going to it she insisted on coming, but promised Roy not to heckle or cause a scene. Roy made it clear that he would not be able to show us much attention at the meeting or hobnob with us afterwards, when he would be talking to the leaders of the Swindon Labour Party.

The three of us took up our positions in the Swindon Town Hall as discreetly as we could, but I couldn't help thinking that Ann, dressed in her fur coat, stood out – the opposite of the proverbial sore thumb – among the hundreds of soberly dressed Labour members. The name of the Labour candidate in the election was placarded round the walls in red and yellow. I was on the point of telling Alexandra, whose first political meeting it was, that it reminded me of a similar pre-war gathering except that there was less excitement at the entrance, when Roy steamed confidently up the aisle, surrounded by a convoy of local Party officials. The three of us nudged each other conspiratorially.

When Roy stood up to speak, I thought how suitable for a leading politician it was to have the corporation with which he was now generously endowed. There was nothing lean or hungry about him. He had *gravitas*. With considerable verve he gave a eulogistic account of the Government's achievements and of the qualities of the Labour candidate. He dealt with aplomb with interruptions by one or two hecklers. He deplored Swindon's aberration in having elected a Tory at the previous election. In answer to a question about education, he said with a confident sweep of the arm that the matter was covered by the Robbins target. 'What's the Robbins target?' I asked Ann. 'I've no idea,' she answered, adding in her staccato Charteris way, 'but I'll never forget it.' We behaved ourselves impeccably until Roy started talking about the budget and the need for keeping expenditure within income for the country, as for the family. 'We all know', he declared, 'that in the family budget if you spend more than you can earn, and if you spend more on food than you can afford, you soon get into trouble...' This interjection about food led to commotion and shaking between us that would have registered high on any Richter scale.

When he finished speaking, Roy was given a long round of applause. The chairman thanked him for his speech and for everything he had done for the Party. He then announced that the time had come for all present to make a contribution. Collecting-boxes would be coming round and everyone was asked to give as generously as possible towards funds for the Labour Party.

'This is our moment to leave,' said Ann, rising to her feet. I hesitated, saying that it might be rather conspicuous if we all got up to go at that moment. Ann was insistent that she had to get home for dinner and that she had to leave immediately. 'Oh Nicko,' she protested, 'you're such a diplomat!' However, rather weakly if possibly wisely, I withdrew with her, and Alexandra followed. We edged our way out of the hall, evading the collecting-boxes.

We all met for lunch the following day at The White Hart in Hamstead Marshall, a restaurant which was accorded star treatment in *The Good Food Guide*. Most of the clientele, comprising wealthy landowners and commuters from the Newbury area, were probably Tory voters.

'Roy's more likely to get eggs thrown at him here than in the Swindon Town Hall,' I suggested to Ann as we arrived. 'Yes,' she replied, 'but they will be *oeufs en cocotte*, much more suitable for our Roy than raw eggs.'

The stream of time has rolled on for nearly twenty years since Ann died, yet her friends remember and miss her, not for any important post she held or for any particular achievement, but for such incidents of incongruity as this that brought surprise and amusement to their lives. Although a Tory of the deepest blue she had in later years come to draw many of her friends from the upper reaches of the Labour Party. They were the ones in power; besides which, while her character was consistent, her interests had changed and she found the Labour members more stimulating than those of her earlier White's world.

She had the conventional uneducated upbringing of girls of the upper classes. Much of her youth was spent at Stanway, the beautiful Cotswold-stone house of her grandparents, who were central figures in the Souls, an élite of aristocrats communing much with each other to stem the rising tide of philistinism. There, largely under the influence of her father, she acquired the love of wild-flowers and birds that was to remain an enduring passion whatever the vicissitudes of her life. She herself did not revolt against her background; she was defiant and courageous by nature but not rebellious. However, early on, she evidently began to feel the need to protest against conformity, when she wrote in her diary after her coming-out party: 'Why do I like cads and bounders?'

In retrospect she is often talked about as a great hostess, and as someone who has had no comparable successor. It is certainly true that, alas, there is no one nowadays who entertains in the style she did. But she was not a political hostess, as was her contemporary, Pamela Berry, nor did she aim at collecting and displaying celebrities after the fashion, somewhat earlier, of Emerald

Cunard. She gathered together people of different but original views and she liked to provoke argument, and to stir things up recklessly, which had the effect of making everyone feel more alive. Her guests came away feeling not crushed but stimulated. Noël Annan has likened her in naval terms to a privateer: 'She would move into a calm lagoon where barques and frigates were careening peacefully and suddenly loose off a broadside. The calm vanished, ripples spread across the waters, the whole harbour became animated, galvanised, expectant.' I, on the other hand, saw her more in a rural than a nautical setting: all would be still and sombre in a river valley, except for the murmur of the current and the occasional squawk of a duck, when all at once there would be a brilliant shaft of colour and a splash as a kingfisher dived into the water and emerged with its prey. Her features were sharp, her repartee and movements quick, her personality mercurial.

I didn't get to know her until she was nearly forty when, in 1952, she had just married Ian Fleming, her third husband, whom, appropriately, she had first met at Le Touquet many years before. As she has recorded, she had dined with him the night before her wedding to Esmond Rothermere in 1945. They walked and talked in the park afterwards and she would have accepted had he suggested marriage. Their feelings for each other rarely synchronised. He had declared his love for her over Christmas in 1941, which she regarded as 'a damned inconvenient moment'. It was characteristic of her wayward romanticism, and of her frankness about it, that she told me many years later how, when she went to Tony Crosland's house for her first assignation with Hugh Gaitskell, and Tony opened the door to her, she was so instantaneously taken with him that she would have chosen him for an affair rather than Hugh, had he asked.

Ann's and Ian's interests and tastes increasingly diverged. He liked golf and technical experts, the latter exemplified by metal-buffers, so he told me. He complained that Ann only saw people who lived within a square mile of Victoria Square. True, they may have been geographically confined, but there was no limit to the variety of the company she kept for her glittering parties in her corner house with bow windows looking on to that square. These comprised *inter alia*: artists (Lucian Freud and Francis Bacon); writers (including, as frequent guests, Noël Coward, Evelyn Waugh, Cyril Connolly, Anthony Powell, Stephen Spender, Paddy Leigh Fermor and Peter Quennell); academics, of whom John Sparrow, Isaiah Berlin, Noël Annan and Maurice Bowra spring to mind; grandees, such as the Devonshires, the Lambtons, the Charterises, and the Duff Coopers; an occasional surprise like Greta Garbo; not to mention Ann's new world of high-minded politicians and journalists, including Roy and Jennifer Jenkins, Mark and Leslie Bonham Carter, Robert Kee, the Grimonds and, of course, the Gaitskells.

The leitmotif of Ann's entertainments was pleasure. Her guests were there to enjoy themselves. They certainly did, thanks to the stimulus of the company, the style of her interior decoration and the food, which was original without being elaborate. I recall in particular the cheese ice-cream, the recipe for which came from her favourite work on food and drink, *Lady Sysonby's Cook Book*, which the author described as being for good plain cooks who have never been chefs. It had an introduction by Osbert Lancaster and decorations by Oliver Messel.

Ian did not share in the enjoyment. He would enter the house as the evening started, take a look at the company and then retire to his room on the top floor for the rest of the evening.

Ann was not dazzled by Ian's sudden world-wide fame as the author of James Bond. She was not an admirer of his books. She was not attracted to the actor who played James Bond in the films. She did not share Ian's taste in art, particularly his bronzes. She was not amused by being driven in his sports car, which he had bought with the proceeds from the sale of one of his early best-sellers.

After we had been posted to the Embassy in Vienna, Ian and Ann came there in Thunderbird (the name of his Ford). Thunderbird became the sobriquet by which Ian was known to his friends. Ann arrived with a crick in her neck and a severe cold, as a result of exposure to the elements in Thunderbird. She did not take kindly to the way Ian spent his time in Vienna immured in his hotel bedroom with a nubile blonde secretary, to whom he dictated his new novel.

Talking to me many years later, Ann told me of a dinner she and Ian had arranged to have together in some restaurant to try to improve their relations. They had agreed that each would say with the utmost frankness what they regarded as the main faults in the other. What happened was that Ian took so long to describe Ann's failings that she had no time to expose his, before they were both exhausted.

Gaitskell died before Ian. Given that Gaitskell was then Labour Leader of the Opposition, it was astonishing that his liaison with Ann, although widely known in the circles they frequented, was never publicised by the media. But the discretion then, compared with nowadays, of the press as regards politicians is yet another example of the change that has come over public life.

After Ian's death in 1964 Arnold Goodman became an important figure in Ann's life. They made an incongruous couple. She remained slim and elegant, he was neither. Laura Grimond put him in the category of child-frighteners on account of his appearance. He helped Ann with her finances and, like so many, noticeably those who were least like her in character, he was bewitched by her wit and courage. As in her relations with Rothermere and Fleming, so with Goodman: synchronisation was lacking at the crucial moments. He proposed marriage to her, something he had not done to anyone else, but she did not accept. Later she may have been inclined to do so but the proposal did not come again.

Ann was an animator – one of those people who enhance the vitality of others without wishing to dominate the scene themselves. She was certainly that, but at heart I remember her, not for her witty retorts in Victoria Square, nor for her sparkling presence at great receptions in marble halls, but at Sevenhampton, her house in Wiltshire, where she spent much time in her last years. She was happy there in close friendship with one or two, rather than a crowd. She loved to look out upon the sloping expanse of lawn and the lake that was somewhat melancholy but where the sedge had not withered and the birds sang. That to me was her true element.

11

TO KURDISTAN WITH CY SULZBERGER

'Why don't you come trout-fishing with me in Kurdistan?' Cy Sulzberger[1] asked me one day when I was having lunch with him at the Lucas Carton restaurant in Paris. I was taken with the idea, having recently begun fishing with the enthusiasm of a novice; and I also liked the thought of Cy as a companion. So, I accepted.

A nephew of the proprietor of the *New York Times*, Cy had for years written a column for the paper on the strength of lightning visits to political and military leaders throughout the world. Hard-hitting and hard-drinking, with flashing eyes and a forceful personality, but rough and ready in manner and attire, Cy always wore a wartime bush-shirt off duty, a garment that symbolised his character. His manner of work as a newspaper correspondent was to arrive by air in some capital, set himself up in the US Embassy or local Hilton, order a stiff whisky and then telephone the office of the head of state or of government to ask for a meeting.

---

1 Cyrus Sulzberger, 1912–1993, journalist whose column appeared three times a week in the *New York Times*.

Cy Sulzberger fishing in Kurdistan.

They would invariably agree. After the meeting Cy would return to the hotel, type out his report and send it off to the paper, where it would soon appear. When published it would immediately arouse indignation among the leaders of the country he had written about because Cy did not go in for pussy-footing journalism. But whatever their wrath, it made them not a whit less ready to see him when he next turned up. After all, the USA was the dominant force in the world; the US press had global influence, and the *New York Times* was seen abroad as its lodestar.

After seeing Harold Wilson in 1964, soon after he became Prime Minister, Cy described him in an article as having the face of a halibut and the eyes of a shark. He received much angry mail, not from people complaining that he had insulted the Prime

Minister, but from ichthyologists protesting that Wilson had blue eyes, which sharks never have.

By the time of this lunch with me in Paris, Marina, his scintillating Greek wife, was dead, and his children were abroad. The focus of his home life was his dog, a beagle, which he took everywhere. At our lunch he insisted on giving him some of our *Carotte Vichyssoise*, one of the *spécialités de la maison*.

Cy's chosen relaxations were poker and hard liquor. The company he liked to keep was that of service chiefs. His favourite military leader at this time was General Lauris Norstad, Supreme Allied Commander in Europe, and it was Norstad's enthusiasm, and, as I came to realise in retrospect, the imprecision of his accounts of the fishing, that had led to our expedition to Kurdistan and to the unexpected turn taken by our sport there. It was also thanks to Norstad that we became the guests of Kamran Inan, a senator from Eastern Turkey.

Parisian friends were astonished that we should be going so far for such an accessible fish as trout. Some expressed alarm, for were not the Kurds an unruly and bellicose people who only recently had shown their hostility to Western visitors, and what about snakes and wild animals? But of course for us, in our sheltered lives, the hazard was half the point; and anyway, we had infinite faith in the Turkish senator's protection.

Accompanied by a young interpreter from the Turkish Foreign Ministry called Ōmür Sũlendil (his first name pronounced like that of Bulldog Drummond's adversary, Irma) we flew a thousand kilometres east from Ankara to Lake Van. There we were received by the local governor and driven in trucks, escorted by various attendants, to our destination, a valley called Bahçesaray, some two and a half hours over the mountains south-east towards the Iraq frontier.

Our drive was spectacular, for the first hour and a half winding up and round increasingly barren mountains. We passed one small stream and speculated about the size of trout it might contain. We raised the subject gingerly with the governor, a smiling man who reminded us of a genial and youthful Marshal Tito. His response was disconcerting. Small trout, so he pronounced, tasted better than big ones; a remark that both of us sensed to be as discouraging as it was untrue.

We climbed higher and higher to the pass at 10,000 feet. Dry as a desert. No sign of vegetation or of birds or wild animals. 'Reminds me', said Cy, 'of those photos of Alan Shepherd playing golf on the moon.' I said that the governor and all those accompanying us to our mysterious fishing destination clearly thought us nuts. 'Perhaps they're right,' said Cy.

From the moment we started our descent down a precipitous dust road, with a vertical drop of hundreds of feet on one side, there were signs of life: at first a bird or two, then wild flowers – thyme, lavender and white opium poppies – and, as we wound our way down, springs of water bursting out of the mountain side. Thousands of feet below we caught sight of a carpet of trees and pasture, and of the river we were making for, which was the main source of the Tigris. It looked like a sheet of lightning.

Suddenly we saw three blue tents pitched among some young poplars near the river. 'Paradise,' I said. 'Looks to me like toilets at a chrysanthemum show,' said Cy. There was truth in both remarks, the beauty of tents, even more than of most things, being in the eye of the beholder. We soon installed ourselves in them.

Each tent was equipped with a camp-bed, table and carpet, gauze windows and a zip-fastener front door. A hundred yards away a privy, that would not have looked out of place in a Bolshoi stage-set for *Giselle*, had been constructed for us out of poplar planks. No grand vizier, I felt sure, could have been better treated on safari, and Peter Fleming would have turned up his nose at such luxury.

Cy had travelled with an enormous trunk that had caused us problems throughout the journey and that could only with difficulty be accommodated in his tent. It contained little except for the inevitable bush-shirts, and I asked him why he had not used something smaller, to which he replied typically that, as he possessed this trunk, he saw no reason to buy anything else.

The governor departed. He left the Kurdish chief of the nearby village, Orhan Aýhan, to look after us. As we ate dinner outside by the light of a Coleman lamp, he told us that a few weeks earlier a terrific hailstorm had hit the valley. This had produced a high wall of water that had carried off all the fish. He deplored our luck but doubted whether in any case we would have caught fish with the rods, lines and flies we were proposing to use. He told us that there were still fish to be found in the smaller tributaries flowing into our river. 'But we get them a different way,' he explained, 'with the help of lamps and harpoons at night. We'll get you some tonight so that you can see.'

Sure enough, as we breakfasted next morning a dozen trout of about half a pound each were produced. 'You see, there are fish,' Orhan declared. Cy opened up two of them and declared with Sherlock Holmes-like authority that they were both female and that the stomach of one was full of grasshoppers. 'You'd better choose flies that look like grasshoppers,' he instructed me.

After a delicious breakfast of local honey and cheese we began fishing in earnest. We had no luck in the river near the camp. I decided to walk downstream in the hope that the fish there would have been less affected by the famous hailstorm. The landscape was magnificent: bare mountains beneath a lapis lazuli sky; walnut and willow trees, thick crops of clover, alfalfa, potatoes, beans and marijuana; and threading down the middle the turbulent water of our river.

I passed through a little village with flat-topped mud houses and a high mud and brick bridge, known as the Armenian Bridge. Much of the male population seemed to be standing about watching as I photographed the bridge and fished beneath its shade. They appeared friendly but bemused by my antics, expressing their salutations by placing their right hand first to their head, then to their heart. The women were hidden and those that were visible, tending a cow or fetching water, turned away quickly. I learned later that very few visitors from the West, which included Ankara, had ever penetrated to this valley. I was enchanted by everything I saw – but had still had no glimpse of a fish.

When I got back to our camp, rather late for lunch, I found that Cy had had no better luck. Later that evening we decided to try the smaller river where the trout had been harpooned the previous night. Despite strenuous casting, neither of us had the slightest tingle at the end of our lines. But, again, the surroundings were idyllic: giant walnut trees, water bubbling from the mountains, and the air smelling of the hay that lay in Swiss rolls in the fields either side of the river.

Dinner that night was cooked by Orhan's brother and served silently by our guards. We were glad to be seated by the wood fire because the temperature had dropped from 90°F. at midday to below 50°F. We were offered large rounds of unleavened bread folded like pancakes, yoghourt, salad, rice, raw onions, keftedes and shashliks on skewers cut from the poplar trees round the camp. 'The darnedest thing', Cy said as he helped himself to a shashlik, 'is that less than an hour ago I saw them skinning this lamb. I know how long it takes to skin an animal; and there they are, having prepared and cooked the whole animal in a matter of minutes.'

Orhan said that his brother also built bridges and was a poet. Although he could neither read nor write, he could do anything practical. 'You have to be handy in our valley,' he said. 'It is cut off by snow for six months of the year and has no electricity or doctor.' He told us about the flora and fauna, giving the impression that the valley was teeming with wild animals. We paid close attention as he spoke about the snakes, wolves and bears. Hailing from faraway Ankara, Ōmür, sitting there in his incongruously smart city suit, showed interest in, not to say concern about, the bears.

With fishing going so badly we decided one afternoon to down rods and walk up to the source of the Tigris. The water emerged, so we were told, in a great gush hurling itself out of a cave. We set off on foot at about five in the evening – the four of us, Cy, Orhan, Ōmür and I – for the upward trek. Ōmür was particularly excited, telling us that his wife was also called Tigris. He was still wearing his Ankara suit.

We came to a rickety bridge over the river – little more than a hand-made ladder spanning the two banks. It was not level, the gaps between the rungs were uneven and there were no side railings. The water hurtled beneath as if white with fury. Ōműr decided to cross but the rest of us refrained from doing so for fear of falling in.

We were lost in wonderment when we reached the cave – an eruption of water welling up, like milk coming to the boil, and throwing itself over the edge to form the river. The cave was full of rock pigeons, one of which, a baby, had fallen into the water, presumably at the shock of seeing us. We managed to rescue it before the current carried it away.

When we emerged from the cave we caught sight of Ōműr. He was deathly pale, and soaking wet. He shouted that he had fallen in, had been carried away by the current and had nearly drowned. We hurried to his side and he told us how he had hit his head on a rock. He had tried to come back across the river on that flimsy bridge. He'd only been saved by an overhanging willow branch that he had managed to grasp as he was swept down by the river. His Ankara suit, from which water was still seeping, looked as bedraggled as its wearer. He was sure that he was going to catch pneumonia and he felt sick. He was shivering all over. He told us that all his past life had flashed through his mind when he was in the water, so sure was he that he was going to die; and he had thought how lucky it was that his Tigris was pregnant. 'Yes,' I said, 'but why didn't you stay on the other side of the river? Why did you try to cross that bridge again to come back to our side?' Ōműr replied, almost in tears: 'I was afraid I going to be eaten by a bear.'

We never got to the bottom of whether Ōműr had actually seen a bear or whether he had imagined one after listening to the lurid camp-fire talk of the previous evening.

We continued to fish on and off for the next two days but had no joy, as fishermen are apt to say. On our way home through the town of Van, the other side of the mountains, we were welcomed by the governor. He took us to visit the local bazaar where we were immediately confronted at the entrance by an enormous stuffed bear. It was the only one of its kind that Cy and I had caught sight of, but that was more than the sight we had had of any living fish.

12

THE DEVONSHIRES AT HOME

Across the immense arena of the painted hall, we saw Debo and Andrew[1], halfway up the grand stairs, receiving the new arrivals for the Chatsworth Ball. This initial moment of a party, when the guests make their first tentative steps on to the boards of an unfamiliar and highly decorated stage, is apt to set for them the tenor of the whole evening. They are not asking to be made to feel at home. On the contrary, they've left home for a whiff of adventure. They want to be welcomed as players in a strange and dazzling pageant; and this is exactly how Mary and I felt as we reached the house from the nearby hotel where we were staying and walked up the stairs to be greeted by our host and hostess.

Of course, Debo and Andrew are past-masters at this process of initiation: plenty of cordiality and warmth but just the slightest sign of reserve about how it's all going to turn out; not a flicker of indifference but, on the contrary, a hint of being as much ac-

---

1 Andrew, 11th Duke of Devonshire, KG, MC, b. 1920, m. 1941 Hon. Deborah Mitford, DBE, youngest d. of 2nd Baron Redesdale. Their ball was given on 6 July 1990.

The Devonshires at home.

complices as you are in a great occasion and a sense that you're all in it together to make it go. This was certainly the feeling that Debo and Andrew managed to impart, perhaps by a word on the side or by a meaningful glance, as Mary and I shook hands with them on that imposing staircase.

It was impossible to overlook the elegance of their appearance even though I didn't have the necessary *haute couture* knowledge to be able to appraise the particular distinction of Debo's scarlet dress. She told me afterwards that it had been made many years before by Balmain and had been a present from Derek Jackson. I couldn't but admire its splendour, just as I was dazzled by the incomparable glitter of her jewellery. Andrew, who admits to a love of clothes, yet is a follower of Beau Brummel's injunction against all ostentation, managed, as always, to look exceptionally, yet casually, elegant.

We moved into the large drawing-rooms shimmering with the phantasmagoria of evening dresses and the sparkle of diamonds, emeralds and rubies mounted in bracelets, necklaces, earrings and tiaras, many of which had been liberated for the evening from family strongholds. Full-length looking-glasses on opposing walls reflected and replicated the kaleidoscope of colours.

Mingling with the others, the questions 'Who is here?' and 'Who is not here?' that are apt to intrude immediately into all parties were compounded in our minds by a division that had been made in the guest-list between those who had been invited both to the dinner and to the ball and those who had only been invited to the ball. The dinner guests were mostly from three generations of the family, plus a few close friends. It became apparent that nearly all the grandees – dukes, diplomats and millionaires – had been invited only to the ball. This discrimination flattered those of us who found ourselves in the dining category. Besides, as Debo admitted to me, it greatly simplified the seating problem at table.

I overheard a guest, who, from her confident manner and voice, could well have belonged to the Devonshire House set of a bygone age, turn to her neighbour, the renowned leading couturier of France, M. Hubert Givenchy, asking him for his reaction to the finery of the evening. *'Incroyable'* was his answer. He was evidently bowled over by the jewellery, but much less so by the dresses. I don't know how he compared them with those of a ball in France, but I think he was struck by the difference of English chic – less extravagant than the French in the use of satins, taffetas and lace and not governed by fashion or necessarily made just for this grand occasion. Also remarkable was the wide variation in age of the guests. Without inhibition, the younger generations manifested their own interpretation of what a ball-gown should be. Apart from being impressed by the splendour of the jewellery I have an idea that Givenchy was tickled by the way some of the young wore their tiaras, cramming them forward so that they looked like the Fairy Queen in a school play.

On the command of a liveried master of ceremonies we took our seats for dinner in the biggest marquee. This had been magnificently decorated and took in some of the statuary of the park. A *trompe l'oeil* of mountain scenery adorned the side walls. Reality was imparted to the painted landscape by elephantine boulders covered with vegetation, interspersed with wooden gates suggesting the way to some upland pasture. At first sight it looked like Switzerland, but this impression was soon eclipsed by the impact of Neptune bestriding a fountain, a vast statue that dominated the scene. There was no doubt; we were in the Derbyshire of the Bachelor Duke, the 6th Duke of Devonshire.

A procession of parlour-maids bore in the dishes for dinner. The menu started with Cornish lobster, a dish served to the 250 guests, which a neighbour from the county described to me, with the down-to-earth delicacy of the shires, as having set the Duke back a pretty penny.

No lingering at table after dinner was allowed. We were all summoned to the house to join in the gracious greeting of the ball-guests. I introduced our friend Janetta Parladé to one or two people but then lost her in the crowd. This was inevitable given the size of the throng and of the house. Indeed, I can only have seen half the guests throughout the evening. Several days later I was still hearing of people who had been at the party without my having set eyes on them there.

Dancing to carefully chosen thirties music took place in the central courtyard which had been covered for the evening. The very young and the not so young intermingled seamlessly. Many of the former, unlike their elders, wore white tie and tails, which caused Andrew to go out of his way to thank them for having been thus courteous to him. Impressive on the floor was Paddy Leigh Fermor giving a Cretan rendering of a Viennese waltz in partnership with Evangeline Bruce. The corsage of her ball-gown displayed a Victorian brooch of 'trembling diamonds'.

At one stage Mary and I visited the Moroccan tent. It had been lent by Prince Charles and was designed for pop music and late-night dancing. It was arranged with exotic imagery, very far removed from the aura of the adjacent Peak District. Young and old were disporting themselves there in due dervish fashion, afterwards reclining on divans covered with oriental cushions. Illness prevented Prince Charles attending the party, and Princess Diana felt she couldn't come without him. Her absence was a particular blow to the staff who, expecting her to be there, had polished everything up with special vigour and taken great trouble with their uniforms.

We lost account of time in this midsummer night's dream but it must have been around midnight when we were invited outside to watch the fireworks. As we made our way to the lake and the Emperor fountain we were offered tartan rugs to protect us against the night air. We found ourselves accompanied by strange figures. Grotesquely caparisoned creatures walked among us. Pierrots on stilts stalked to and fro. To me they added to the enchantment, but surprisingly Debo didn't like them – so she told me afterwards. Perhaps it was because they upset her favourite dog, Grandpa, who followed her faithfully throughout the evening.

Fireworks started to streak into the sky to the sounds of a loudspeaker relaying Beethoven's Fifth Symphony. The whole welkin was soon alight, as was the lake which reflected the fireworks in the sky. What remained for long on the retina of my mind's eye was the indigo colour of some of the stars thrown out by the rockets as they dived and crackled before suddenly vanishing into thin air. Just when we thought that the display was finished and that there would be no more rockets they started up again, until at last the extravagance was over and the fabulous firmament was dark and quiet, compelling us to applaud loudly, as if we had been watching grand opera. The spell was only broken by the sound of Jimmy Goldsmith's helicopter taking off noisily.

From the fireworks we were invited to breakfast. It was no quick collation, but a three-course meal. I sat next to Elizabeth Cavendish, Andrew's sister. Her boss, Princess Margaret, was seated opposite, but this didn't appear to cramp her style at all. Her style, a Cavendish one, is to buttonhole whoever she is with, to find out what they really think of some topical and preferably controversial subject in which she is interested. 'Nicko,' she asked in her customary direct way, 'what do you think of it all? How long can it all last?' My reaction was pathetic. I didn't know what she was getting at, and I intimated as much. I mumbled some-

thing about it sounding like a tricky subject. Instead of this reticence, I should have seized on her eagerness to discuss anything,
regardless of time and place. In fact, in that bewitching hour and
in the shadow of that historic house, it would have been the ideal
moment to have talked of many things, including sealing-wax,
cabbages and even kings, the hovering presence nearby of HRH
serving, not as an impediment, but as a stimulus.

The Chatsworth Ball may not have compared in grandeur
with the Devonshire House Ball of the end of the nineteenth century or with the 1951 Bestegui Ball in Venice, and, of course, it was
quite different to them in not being in fancy dress. But it was
memorable for many of the young for being the first great dance
that they had attended, and for those of an older generation, because it signified the survival, after long years of neglect and
threat, of the great English country house – a private dwelling, a
treasure house and a social and cultural arena.

13

A PARAGON OF A HOST

Soon after we arrived at Sissinghurst one summer afternoon for the weekend, Nigel Nicolson[1], discussing his father's reputation, said that Harold was not a snob, as so many people nowadays accused him of being, but an élitist. He had not enjoyed the small-talk of diplomacy when he belonged to that profession, nor the run-of-the-mill exchanges obligatory with constituents when he was an MP. What he liked was conversation with people who shared his interests and came from more or less the same background as he did. Swayed by the thought of Harold Nicolson's critical, slightly Epicurean attitude to the outside world, I confessed to the same élitism.

Et in Arcadia ego was how I felt at the prospect of the weekend with Nigel and his friends, as Mary and I made our way across the garden to the cottage where Harold and Vita had had their bed-

---

1 Nigel Nicolson, MBE, FSA, b. 1917, author, son of Harold Nicolson and Vita Sackville-West; served WW2 Grenadier Guards; MP 1952–59, publications include a biography of Field-Marshal Alexander, and, as editor, the diaries of his father and the letters of Virginia Woolf.

Nigel Nicolson at Sissinghurst.

rooms and Harold his study. This was to be our lodging. The study, lined with books and a few personal treasures, such as some lines in Benjamin Constant's hand, gave on to the garden through leaded windows. Harold's desk was an L-shaped pine table-top with bookshelves to the right so that he only had to stretch out a hand to be able to reach any of the much-thumbed volumes of the *Oxford Dictionary*, or of the *Encyclopaedia Britannica*, or of the *DNB*.

One or two trifles from the past still adorned the desk-table, for instance a faded copy, preserved in a plastic folder, of one of his articles from the *Spectator*, republished upon his death in 1968. From a glance I saw that it lamented the impermanence of nature – rose-petals falling – compared with the endurance of inanimate objects such as his typewriter and hole-puncher. He acknowledged the platitudinous nature of his reflections. Both his response to nature and his admission of the banality of his reactions were exactly what mine would have been in similar circumstances. If I had walked round the garden on a sunny summer morning, as he had done before settling down to writing, I would have been moved, as he had been, by the same feelings of ecstasy followed by fatalism; and I would also have realised how unoriginal they were, even if irrepressible.

Seated at Harold Nicolson's desk, my mind was drawn to the intermittent moments when in earlier times our paths had crossed: how he had come to Oxford in the summer of 1940 and had terrified us undergraduates with descriptions of the brutal impact of the Nazi *Blitzkrieg* against France and had then, following his visit, written an article for the *Spectator* saying how much, how painfully closely, the young men he had just seen reminded him of the doomed pre-1914 generation to which he belonged; and how his weekly columns in that paper – witty, self-deprecating, and Francophile – had captured the imagination of many of my contemporaries who were already subjugated by the literary charm of *Some People*.

As Nigel showed us the geography of the cottage, he explained that it was let by the National Trust, which owns the entire Sissinghurst property, to Ed Victor, a successful American literary agent. He allowed it to be used when he was not there. We were told that Stephen Spender and Iris Murdoch had stayed there recently, which obviously enhanced its *cachet*. We were also vouchsafed the literary titbit that the bath, installed by Ed Victor, was so deep that Iris Murdoch had had difficulty in getting out of it. I

had a passing pang of sympathy for Iris, who had been my contemporary at Oxford, and a momentary feeling of doubt concerning Mary's and my bathing prowess. There was clearly no
rope, such as is suspended above each bath in Brooks's, to help
the elderly members extricate themselves.

In a marvellously considerate piece of hospitality, Nigel had
left on the table in the kitchen-dining-room of the cottage some
typed notes to serve as a *vade mecum* for the guests. These included details of the various items we would find there for breakfast, on the likely assumption that we would not want to join the
rest of the party in the castle on that occasion. Most useful and in-
triguing were the biographies Nigel had left for us, giving details
of those staying the weekend and those coming in for meals. They
were highly descriptive. We found later that the guests seemed reluctant to offer to exchange with each other Nigel's pen portraits,
or at any rate to do so with us, which made us wonder. I think that
this hidden agenda gave a slight *frisson* to Nigel's enjoyment of
the weekend. He himself was sensitive to his guests' possible reaction to the envelope containing these biographical notes but not
in the way one would expect. The following message accompanied it: 'If you don't want to know in advance (some people think
this habit of mine very strange) tear this up unopened. Nigel.'

The other house-guests included Sue Baring and the Martin
Drurys. New blood was brought in for dinner – the Jim Roses,
and the Christopher Hudsons. A writer for the *Daily Telegraph*
under the name Kirsty Mcleod, Mrs Hudson initiated what
turned out to be lively argument on Anglo-French relations. I am
glad to say that, led passionately by Pam Rose, the Francophiles
won. Drue Heinz was expected but failed to turn up that evening.

When she did arrive the following day, nobody saw fit to ask what had happened, knowing, as we all did, that, like the Scarlet Pimpernel, she is elusive concerning her whereabouts. Her presence was missed because, as I was aware, having accompanied her to many lectures, she loves discussion – the more animated the better.

The National Trust obviously has responsibility for the maintenance of the garden, but I sensed that Nigel's continuing presence makes it feel as though it belongs to a person, not to an institution. This is so despite the stream of visitors and the passage of time since the creators, Vita and Harold, lived there. He had provided the structure, she the planting. Members of the public seem to walk about in it as if they feel at home there too, and, astonishingly, they don't make it appear like a public place. Anticipating the promise of later private and privileged access to the garden, Mary and I were unable to resist rushing out at the first opportunity and joining in the public throng. We admired the legibility of the plant labels. We were impressed by the riotous abundance of the flowerbeds contrasted with the strict order of the paths and avenues, and by the exuberance of colour and scent within very strict patterns.

In pouring rain on Saturday afternoon, Nigel took us to see the famous garden at Great Dixter and to meet its owner, the formidable and notoriously unpredictable Christopher Lloyd. He showed us over his house, particularly the Lutyens additions. Mary explained her interest, derived from having lived in Lutyens' Embassy in Washington. This left him quite unmoved. Nevertheless, he seemed readier to get on with Mary than with the rest of us, who were invariably subjected to crushing retorts.

Admittedly, at one moment I had asked for it. Before setting out for Great Dixter we had all been glancing at a book on the subject of building bricks written by Christopher Lloyd's father. When, at his house, Christopher pointed to some building and mentioned the name Lloyd as architect, I said, in somewhat ingratiating fashion: 'Oh, that's your father who wrote about bricks,' to which he snapped back, 'Yes; I only had one father.'

In fact Mary was just as oleaginous as the rest of us without, however, engendering his sarcasm, much to our annoyance; but we were all amused later in exchanging details of the snubs we had suffered – and which in retrospect we enjoyed.

Despite the rain, we were able to admire Lloyd's garden, notably the topiary. Nigel said that it was a plantsman's garden. As evidenced in Lloyd's regular columns in *Country Life*, it was of particular concern to botanists, whereas at Sissinghurst the emphasis was on the way plants were arranged and displayed in the interests of those looking at them.

To his unconcealed annoyance, I took a photograph of Lloyd wearing a cone-cap that he said dated from his school-days. He was clearly suspicious that I was intending to publish it. Martin Drury said that he didn't think any photo of Lloyd had ever been published.

Later, I asked Nigel about Vita's relations with Lloyd. Did they regard themselves as rivals? He said that they trod warily round each other. The mental picture of the circumambulation of this uncompromising couple tickled me considerably.

Early the next morning Mary and I were to experience another example of Nigel's hospitality: he had arranged for the Sunday papers to be left outside the door of the cottage. We paid them deservedly scant notice before devoting serious attention to Sissinghurst's outdoor rooms, as Vita called them. It so happened that we had recently seen several varied but magnificent gardens: Chatsworth, Crathes, Cholmondeley Castle and Hatfield, not to mention David Hicks's recent creation. We were not to make comparisons. Mary hates my tendency to do this, to say of one place that it reminds me in some way of another, but she joined me in recognising and revelling in the unique quality Sissinghurst has of appealing to all the senses and enveloping one in complete peace.

The large buffet lunch on Sunday was dominated by Denis Healey who was his usual boisterous self. We ate outside and I decided that Denis was at his best in unconfined surroundings. With Edna, as always, I had a sympathetic time with nostalgic dips into our shared Oxford past.

As we drove home from this perfect weekend I recalled a surprising remark made by one of the lunch guests, that Nigel's brother, Ben, had been more suited than Nigel to social life and entertaining. So far as we had observed and experienced it, Nigel had shown himself to be a paragon of a host.

14

LISTENING TO
ISAIAH BERLIN

1 The Wardenship of All Souls

'No,' said Isaiah Berlin[1]. 'It would have been quite impossible that I should ever have been elected Warden of All Souls. A Jew? No, quite impossible.'

We were discussing the subject of the election to the wardenship following Humphrey Sumner's death in 1950. This was many years after the election had taken place but Isaiah was evidently eager to talk to me about it when I visited him one day in his house at Headington.

He had been a candidate, 'a reluctant one,' he said, 'and your father also, though even more reluctant.' A.L. Rowse had resorted to various machinations in an effort to have Eric Beckett elected.

---

1 Sir Isaiah Berlin, OM, CBE, 1909–1997, philosopher and author; President British Academy; Fellow of All Souls Coll. Oxford and New Coll. Oxford; m. Aline de Gunzbourg; war service, Ministry of Information, New York and the British Embassy Washington; Professor Social and Political Theory, Oxford; President Wolfson College Oxford; publications include: *Karl Marx; The Hedgehog and the Fox; Russian Thinkers; Against the Current; Personal Impressions.*

Isaiah Berlin.

Beckett, the legal adviser in the Foreign Office, was someone, said Isaiah, whom Rowse had thought he would be able to control completely. Isaiah analysed the attitudes and voting strength of the younger fellows, most of whom, he thought, would have chosen him. 'But', he said, 'Brand backed your father and this eventually triumphed.'

It turned out to be a tragedy because my father soon fell ill and had to resign, which meant another election. Isaiah felt, I believe, that having stood and been beaten he couldn't very well stand again so soon. As a result, John Sparrow was elected and remained warden for the next thirty years.

Having explained his own abortive candidacy, Isaiah proceeded to a discussion of John Sparrow's character, applying to it the dialectical skill, wit and mimicry that I have known him devote to the analysis of great historical figures. 'John Sparrow', he said, 'is interested in three things: himself, sex and, a long way third, poetry and books. He's not interested in the college. He's not interested in things of the mind. No, he's not a megalomaniac. He doesn't have a very high opinion of himself. But he's introspective, and a deeply unhappy man.'

Isaiah's flow of language was so strong that there was no need for me to give him any encouragement to continue on a theme to which he had obviously given thought. He went on: 'He's excellent company, not in the least a bore. But don't expect a general, highbrow discussion. His idea of Oxford is that of Sligger Urquhart – quite impossible today. He would resign, yes, I say it definitely, Sparrow would resign if women were ever to be admitted to All Souls. He's concerned with things of no practical use, for instance he's become an expert on some seventeenth-century Polish poet who wrote in Latin. He's a very clever man, but not one who wants to think or talk of ideas.'

The words would have continued to tumble out uninterruptedly, but I interjected a question about how Sparrow compared, and got on, with other fellows of the college. 'I mean', he explained, following his own train of thought, 'if you said to Denis Rickett – and I'm taking a very extreme case – that so and so had some new theory, he would reply: "Really?" and be somewhat interested in it, not very, but fairly. But not Sparrow. He likes gossip, and to hear about violence and perversion. Politically, of course, very reactionary – a Powellite.'

ıı A Philosopher's Stroll

'When people ask me what I do, I reply, "Nothing"', Isaiah said *à propos* of no particular subject when we were putting on our coats before walking back from the Garrick where we had been lunching together.

I said: 'I saw your step-grandson the other day in Paris – young Strauss – and he asked me about your sex-life.' '"Lurid" I hope you answered.' To which I replied, 'I told him I'd known you for a long time.' Isaiah then asked me how and when we had first met – which in fact was at Oxford in the mid-thirties.

He looked along the clothes-hooks for his hat. He chose the wrong one, and, as we descended the steps into Garrick Street, he discovered his error and, in some anxiety, returned to the hooks as if in search of a lost child.

As we sauntered towards St Martin's Lane I commented on the elaborate and alluring elevations of the tall Victorian buildings, and, more generally, on the charms of this part of London. 'Yes, yes,' Isaiah bumbled, not dismissively, but as if it were self-evident.

'I suppose we could go via Chinatown,' I said. Isaiah gave a grunt of approval and we set off towards Charing Cross Road, which we agreed, as we crossed it, was not what it was when it enjoyed the reputation of a book-browsers' paradise. Isaiah is a keen browser, not just of books. Someone once told me of an hour or two he had spent with Isaiah browsing amongst the medicines in John Bell and Croyden in Wigmore Street, a passion that may reflect his tendency to hypochondria; but also his love of shopping.

He alluded to this love later in our walk when we came to an ironmonger's shop whose windows were full of paints, coils of string and hand-tools. Isaiah stared at the window with rapt attention as if he were contemplating a display in some oriental *souk*. I suggested we should enter. He replied that he wanted to buy a rubber tip for the end of his umbrella, which he then lifted up to show me. We entered the shop and he was immediately taken by the array of little wooden drawers behind the counter, each bearing a label. He seemed to be in no hurry to indicate his intended purchase. Nor did the shopkeeper show any impatience. Nevertheless, I thought that between us we ought to show some purchasing spirit, so I decided to buy a small oil-can. Isaiah then gave an eloquent description of what he wanted to buy, upon which drawer upon drawer was laid on the counter, each opened in turn, and the contents rummaged in an effort to find an umbrella-tip of exactly the right size. It was not to be found; but Isaiah, enchanted by the drawers, was determined to buy something, so he explained that he had a walking stick at home and that he would like to find a rubber-tip for that. The shopkeeper enquired about the size, which was obviously difficult to determine, so he held out for selection handfuls of different tips. Isaiah said that he would buy six of them so as to be sure of having one at any rate that fitted. As they were being wrapped up, Isaiah produced his wallet, which was bulging with new, crisp notes.

While this transaction, which was far from hurried, was taking place, I asked him whether he had enjoyed his lunch, to which he replied emphatically: 'Yes, very much, especially the walk; and I love shopping.'

He seemed to take a fancy to Chinatown, and, catching sight of some porcelain in a shop window, he scurried over to it, saying 'I'd like to buy something.' But on closer inspection he changed his mind. We passed boxes of strange-looking prickly fruits, piled high on the pavement, and I suggested that Aline, his wife, might be pleased if he bought one for her. He thought not. On reflection, I had to agree. He was right.

On the other side of Shaftesbury Avenue we entered Soho. He appeared to be delighted by the mountains of fruits on the wooden barrows that lined the narrow streets, and by the glittering lights that could be seen above, proclaiming Raymond's Revue Bar. He walked very slowly, apparently taking it all in. We stopped opposite a shop selling old newspapers and film and jazz posters. Commenting on the busts in the window, he said 'There's always one of Beethoven.' We passed a shop that specialised in goods for left-handed people, which excited some curiosity in him. Then, we came to a double window sporting ladies underwear, much of it of leather and all of it black and shining. This also absorbed Isaiah's attention, but, uncharacteristically, he appeared lost for words.

Strolling on, we started a conversation on the subject of intelligence. 'You know,' he said, 'Keith Joseph didn't understand anything about people.' To which I retorted tritely that I thought some very clever people were like that. From which he went on to say something that would have surprised all those, and they are many, who regard him as the cleverest person they have ever met. 'You know, I was never top of my form at school. Sometimes second. Never top.'

Very slowly, as if reluctant to reach the end of our journey, we crossed Regent Street and made our way to the back-door of Albany. Isaiah reached in his pocket for his keys, making sure that his purchases were still there, and let himself in through the secret entrance.

15

MRS THATCHER AND
THE CHANNEL TUNNEL

An event occurred on Boxing Day, 1984, that for a time affected
the course of my life and touched on an issue of some national
and international importance. Mary and I were lunching at Chequers, as we were invited to do on Boxing Day for many years, and
Margaret Thatcher, as was her custom on these occasions, took
me aside for a chat about the international scene. This soon
turned into a chance for the PM to let off steam. She was very
worked up about Star Wars and her recent meeting with President Reagan in which that subject had been predominant. But I
managed to get a word in edgeways and to raise a matter that was
of acute interest to me: her attitude to the project, in which I was
becoming increasingly involved, of a fixed Channel link.

These Yuletide lunches at Chequers often seemed to serve as
opportunities for Mrs Thatcher to unwind and to give vent to
pent-up indignation, in the presence of sympathetic company.
The storm the previous year had raged over President Reagan's
invasion of Grenada – a Commonwealth country – without her
concurrence. The guests at her table had been astonished by her

Mrs Thatcher and President Mitterrand, at Lille, 20 January 1986, to authorise the building of the Channel Tunnel.

irrepressible bitterness and by her frankness in expostulating about the unpredictability in general of the Americans. In both sorrow and anger she had complained to me after lunch that she had always backed Reagan to such an extent that she was often accused of being his cipher. She thought he must consider that he could take her for granted and that she would always back him. She had disagreed with him about the oil pipeline issue and over the Middle East. He had been wrong to throw in his lot so entirely with the Jews and to treat the Arabs with contempt. Reverting to the Grenada affair, she asked me several times how she could prevent what she described as deceit occurring again. My effort to console her, which was all I thought I could do in the circumstances, had been to try to reassure her that Reagan really did mind what she thought. I also said, somewhat simplistically, that nothing would change him, and that, as he was going to be there another five years, the only course would be to hang around and do the best with what you'd got, which was what he was.

This outburst was mild compared with the fury aroused a few years later over President Reagan's meeting with Gorbachev at Reykjavik. 'He almost gave away the store,' she declared to her Boxing Day guests at Chequers, adding: 'What luck that Gorbachev didn't accept.' In an aside, she told me with glee of an account that Bryan Cartledge, HM Ambassador, Moscow, had sent of a recent interview with Gorbachev. He reported that Gorbachev had complained that she, Mrs Thatcher, treated both him and President Reagan like naughty schoolboys.

But although at this and other Boxing Day parties time was taken out for indignation, it in no way interfered with Mrs Thatcher's exceptional courtesy. However much she may have changed during her years in office in her political persona, she remained, at any rate so far as I could judge, constant and considerate to those working close to her; and she was invariably attentive and welcoming to her guests. She never gave them the impression of having little time for them or of exhaustion, even though she had frequently just completed a heavy parliamentary and travel programme. She introduced the guests to each other, without searching for their names; she made sure that they were getting enough to eat and drink from the buffet (usually curried turkey); and, after lunch, she was always ready to show the party over the house, with plenty of historical and cultural detail – too much, some of them may have thought. Denis, who, as the invitation indicated, was joint host, did much to make the guests feel at home.

He was uncannily similar to John Wells's version of him, which somehow affected conversation, making one in turn feel like John Wells.

I was intrigued by the guest-lists at these parties. They didn't suggest any ulterior motive, such as an attempt to reward political support, let alone to gain it. Leading politicians were not numerous and were changed about – some may, of course, have been guests at her more intimate Christmas Day parties. No effort was made to invite a cross-section of national institutions. Much to Number 10's regret, the *Sunday Telegraph* managed to get hold of the list of guests one year, which they published with the comment that it provided no guidance as to who was in and who was out. Why, for instance, was Geoffrey Howe there when everyone knew he was not in favour? The fact, to which they drew attention, that I, a 'passionate European', was on the list, showed that Mrs Thatcher was more tolerant than people gave her credit for. In fact, by the late 1980s, I had been expecting to be dropped from the annual parties on account of the public criticisms I had made of Mrs Thatcher's anti-European policy, but Mary had struck up a special rapport with her over fashion and the rag trade, in which she was greatly interested, and it was probably thanks to this that we survived. Mary, sitting next to Denis at one of the earliest lunches we attended, asked him what they had done over Christmas, to which he replied: 'Well, Margaret and I did our Darby and Joan act on Christmas Day, and now we are enjoying ourselves and relaxing with this party.' They clearly saw Boxing Day as a time to entertain their friends and those they had met recently or who had helped them in some way.

In this last category were the Tommy Sopwiths. Gina was a

first-class skier, undaunted by finding herself off-piste in the political world. He had provided helicopter services for Mrs Thatcher during her electoral campaigns before she became PM. Following her resignation in 1990, she had to cancel the invitations which had already gone out for the usual Boxing Day party, whereupon the Sopwiths gave a lunch for her. I sat next to Carol Thatcher, a freelance journalist, who had frequently been at the Chequers parties. She had always combined a jaunty independence and racy turn of phrase with total loyalty to her mother, and on this occasion she said to me: 'Tory is a four-letter word. They threw out Mum – and I've said so in public.' I would like to have followed this up with more talk about the family's reactions to the resignation, but this was not possible as Mum was sitting opposite. Meanwhile, Denis was explaining his problem of choosing a geographical adjunct to his title of baronet. Having been brought up at Uffington (near the White Horse), he had suggested that name, but those concerned with titles had advised against as it would excite ridicule, so he had settled for a place in Kent.

Reverting to the 1984 Boxing Day party, which, as I have said, proved to be a turning point for me, I listened long while Mrs Thatcher waxed indignant about Star Wars, before managing to seize an opening. 'Prime Minister,' I said, 'changing the subject, there is something I wish to learn from you personally: are you really interested in the idea of a fixed cross-Channel link?' I explained that I was a director of Tarmac, one of the British companies belonging to the Channel Tunnel Group which was putting together a link project. I knew of course of her joint declaration with President Mitterrand the previous November in favour of a link provided it was built by private enterprise and involved no governmental guarantees. But I wanted to know whether she personally was committed to the idea. She replied without hesitation that she believed in it strongly. The only qualification she made was to say that she hoped it would be a drive-through. This was not a scheme the Channel Tunnel Group thought practical. I muttered something to this effect and Mrs Thatcher switched back to Star Wars, but she had said enough to remove any doubt in my mind about her support in principle for a link.

When, therefore, the members of the Channel Tunnel Group asked me shortly afterwards to become their Chairman, I accepted, having been influenced by this sign I had received that Mrs Thatcher was behind the general idea. This *prise de contact* at Chequers also paved the way for me to broach the subject with her in more detail, which I did at a meeting at Number 10 in May 1985. My purpose was to dissuade her from committing herself to a drive-through, which many people in London and Paris were saying she favoured. They were even suggesting that she was dreaming of the day when Denis would be at the wheel taking her on a holiday to France. At our far-from-hurried talk over coffee to the sound of martial music coming from the Trooping the Colour rehearsal in Horseguards Parade, I explained the difficulties and dangers of driving to the Continent on the basis of present technical knowledge. I described how, under our scheme, the traveller would be making the journey. Mrs Thatcher indicated that she now understood what we had in mind. She assured me that she did not favour any particular project but she did feel passionately strongly about the need for some fixed link and considered that the decision must be taken as quickly as possible;

nothing exciting of this kind had been carried out by the British since the end of the Second World War; it was high time we became involved in an industrial enterprise of this scale. It also had highly important implications for our relations with the Continent. She was therefore enthusiastic and would miss no chance of saying so.

I lunched again with Mrs Thatcher at Chequers on Boxing Day 1985, less than a month before the British and French governments were to decide which of the four schemes for a fixed link would receive their mandate. In conspiratorial silence we both avoided the subject, except that she said, crossing her fingers and holding them out before me: 'I'm sure you're doing this.' The following month, the two governments chose our project, and on 29 July 1987 Mrs Thatcher went to Paris to join President Mitterrand in a ceremony marking the exchange of ratifications of the Treaty for a fixed link.

This event provided a small and solemn postscript to my dealings with Mrs Thatcher over the tunnel. Charles Powell, the grand vizier of Mrs Thatcher's Private Office, telephoned me a few days before the ceremony. Could I help him with some ideas and jokes for the speech he was trying to draft for delivery by the PM at the tunnel party? He had already written two speeches for her for tunnel occasions and could think of nothing new to say. Knowing from personal experience the pain of drafting ministerial speeches, I said that I would do my best. Skimming through my commonplace book, which I have often found useful for such purposes, I came across a story that I thought might be suitable, about Hippolyte Taine, the French statesman and historian. Taine specialised in English history and literature. From him, indeed, generations of French people have derived their ideas of the English. But, although an expert in the language, Taine had never managed to master English pronunciation, a shortcoming of which he was happily unaware. Paying an important visit to this country, he was dining in a restaurant and ordered boiled potatoes in a confident voice, not unlike the stentorian tone adopted by some Englishmen when speaking French. Taine was surprised to find himself served with hot buttered toast. I suggested to Charles that he might be able to work this into the speech for Mrs Thatcher whether or not she spoke in French.

Well, there we were in the Elysée for the ceremony, with the TV cameras of the world trained on the President and the PM. When it came to her turn, Mrs Thatcher delivered half her speech in French – and in an impeccable accent. There was no mention of Taine. Charles Powell hastened to my side afterwards and said, 'Sorry about that. The joke was in the speech until midnight, but then, having spent several hours rehearsing her remarks in French so as to get the accent just right, she decided that there was no need to apologise for her pronunciation. So she struck out the joke.' I realised how wrong I had been to imagine that Mrs Thatcher might resort to self-denigration – not her style at all!

Charles went on to say that Mrs Thatcher had learnt the French text phonetically. She didn't speak or understand French. This became apparent immediately after her speech when she was surrounded by French people, including the Prime Minister, Jacques Chirac, who congratulated her in French and asked her to tell them how she had mastered the language. They soon realised that she was quite incapable of carrying on any sort of conversation in French. However, to the rest of the world who had seen the ceremony on television, she had shown a command of the language of which, as the media pointed out, few of her predecessors had been capable.

16

IN HONOUR OF
CENAE LUCULLIANAE

The most bizarre and the most memorable feature for me of the ceremony at the Sheldonian Theatre in Oxford at which, in 1987, I received an honorary degree, was the speech in Latin about my career delivered by the Public Orator, Godfrey Bond.

We, the twelve honorands for doctorates[1], had arrived there literally hot-foot from the Codrington Library, wearing scarlet gowns and floppy hats and watched by crowds full of curiosity, only a little less atwitter than the onlookers had been at the ceremony before the war when P.G. Wodehouse was honoured. None now could match the interest that he had aroused, but the diversity of us honorands, accoutred as we were, and the *gravitas* of the Chancellor of Oxford University, the Right Honourable Lord Jenkins of Hillhead, leading us at a dignified pace and dressed in

---

1 The King of the Belgians, the President of Italy, Dr Garrett Fitzgerald, Dr Alwyn Williams (Vice-Chancellor of Glasgow University), Sir Isaiah Berlin, Dame Iris Murdoch, Professor Dorothy Hodgkin, Mr Robert McNamara, Professor Arthur Schlesinger, Sir Patrick Neill (Vice-Chancellor of Oxford University), Sir Anthony Kenny (Master of Balliol College) and myself.

Degree ceremony at Oxford.

a heavy, golden robe, borne by a page, gave our procession the panoply of a pageant. Entering the Sheldonian, the Chancellor took his seat on what looked like Oxford's idea of a throne; the two heads of state, the King of the Belgians and the President of Italy, were seated on either side of him; the rest of us, who were mere mortals, even if we were about to become doctors, were placed in the aisle.

Referring to my time as Ambassador in Paris, the Public Orator spoke of the entertaining we had done there. It was, according to the translation from Latin, 'a subject on which the ambassador is an expert; for with the help of his wife, who knows about superb cooking, he gave Lucullan feasts (*cenae Lucullianae*), which were famous even in Paris.' Mary was furious about this reference. She regarded it as male chauvinism, suggesting that she should only be recognised for her contribution to the cooking, as though she had spent her whole time in Paris in the kitchen. The correspondent of the *Independent* picked up this Lucullan passage and sent a report on the ceremony which appeared on the front page the following morning. He wrote that at the mention of these dinners in Paris the otherwise impassive features of the chancellor manifested, discreetly but unmistakably, a fleeting display of emotion.

A new chancellor of Oxford University has a moment of glorious patronage when, on assuming office, he can put forward his own list of twelve candidates for honorary doctorates. When Roy Jenkins told me in June 1987 of his decision to include me in his list I considered it more gratifying than any other honour I had been given. Soon afterwards I received a letter from the Registrar of the University, Dr A.J. Dovey. He expressed pleasure that I had agreed that 'the University's Chancellor-elect would be proposing to the University that the Degree of Doctor of Civil Law, *honoris causa*, be conferred upon you at a special ceremony on the 20th October, to mark the start of Mr Jenkins' Chancellorship'. The letter went on to say that in accordance with usual practice 'proposed nominations would be treated as confidential until they could all be published together in the University Gazette, for consideration by Congregation, where the statutes of the University permit a vote to be requested'.

Two weeks later, the Registrar wrote saying that he was glad to be able to tell me that Congregation had approved the proposal to confer the degree upon me. Details of the programme for the 20 October ceremony would shortly be sent to me by the Vice-Chancellor's secretary. In early September, a letter arrived from the Vice-Chancellor's secretary asking me for details of my height and hat-size, necessary for the provision of the appropriate academic robe and headgear to be worn at the *Encaenia* degree ceremony. She also sent an outline of the proceedings on 20 October which included instructions on when I should wear my doctor's hood and gown.

In recording all this, I have to interject that the sheer pomp and formality of the degree-giving procedure have the effect of bolstering the self-esteem of the recipient, by now no doubt a little attenuated by years in the shadows of retirement, however prolix and tiresome the whole rigmarole may seem to those not honoured.

Sure enough, within two weeks I received a letter from Geoffrey Warnock, Principal of Hertford College, where I was an honorary fellow. He was delighted that my name was 'among the new Chancellor's bisques for honorary degrees … which', he was glad to say, 'had gone through Congregation without controversy!' The exclamation mark conveyed relief that the discord that had arisen in Oxford over the proposal to give Mrs Thatcher an honorary degree had not been repeated. Warnock concluded his letter by offering to serve as 'a base for the goings on on the 20th October', an invitation I accepted gratefully.

Mary and I drove to Oxford the evening before the ceremony. We were to attend a pre-*Encaenia* dinner at the Isaiah Berlins, which was being given mainly for the visiting Americans: Bob McNamara and Arthur Schlesinger, both about to receive degrees; and Marietta Tree, Joe Alsop and Kay Graham, close friends. The Roy Jenkinses were also present. Aline Berlin responded to the epicurean tastes of the company by serving a sumptuous dinner and a 1945 Château Lafite. We had general conversation at the round table, devoted not to any profound subject, but, much of it, to Isaiah's favourite theme of making lists. The list that held the attention of the table the longest was of people who were bogus, a quality accorded particular censure in the canon of Oxford since the time of Maurice Bowra. It was agreed that the British outdid the Americans in this roll-call of pseuds. There was a secondary list of creeps, in which the British again more than held their own. The American guests, being nicer and less critically motivated than the British, except for Joe Alsop, were not so ready with names but were no less enthusiastic as an audience in this popular pastime of some of the top brains of Britain.

We spent the night with the Warnocks in Hertford, waking up on the morning of the ceremony to rain. This continued all day. I was sitting downstairs after breakfast when Geoffrey Warnock told me that the Public Orator would shortly be arriving to pay me a courtesy call. In answer to my enquiries, Godfrey Bond explained in precise and modest language how he had mastered the task of compressing into a few lines the essential features of the careers of the twelve honorands, and translating into Latin the scientific achievements of Dame Dorothy Hodgkin. He had spent much time in the Bodleian Library studying their *curricula vitae* and had read several of their books. I was impressed by the thought of this eminent classicist spending hours in the library poring over Iris Murdoch's novels, Isaiah Berlin's history of philosophical thought and Dorothy Hodgkin's Nobel-Prize-winning ideas in chemistry. I thanked him profusely for the trouble he had taken to visit me before the *Encaenia*. It was, I realised, yet another example of the trouble Oxford takes to make the granting of an honorary degree a flattering and far from routine event for the recipient.

The first engagement of the day was the lunch – for 124 people

– in the Codrington Library. Those being honoured had to wear their scarlet gowns and to carry their pliant headgear. The Codrington is a magnificent room, more like a picture gallery, serving as both a library and a place for ceremonious entertaining. I could well remember the many soporific afternoons I had spent there as an undergraduate in the shadow of the statue of the benefactor, Sir Christopher Codrington, with a legal textbook before me, and my attention inclined to wander in the direction of the other more studious students around me – unless I was actually asleep.

At lunch I was seated between Mary Warnock and Kay Graham. Both soon revealed to me that they were having trouble with their other neighbours at table. Dorothy Hodgkin, who was opposite me, seemed to be in the same predicament so the obvious course was to encourage a triangular conversation between the three of them. Kay was eager to know whether being a woman had been a handicap to either Dorothy Hodgkin or Mary Warnock in their distinguished careers. They both answered negatively; indeed they thought that it had been a positive advantage. This three-dimensional cross-table talk continued quite satisfactorily but the suspicion dawned on me that neither of the other two knew exactly who Kay was. I was reminded of the time, many years before, when I was living in France and Kay and Ted Heath had left a conference they were attending to come to Paris for an opera; he had been fêted at some party to which they had both been invited but nobody knew who Kay was, which understandably made her feel out of it, and Ted did nothing to help introduce her. Such is the gap in name-recognition between the two sides of the Atlantic.

Loup flambé au fenouil
Contre-filet a l'anglaise
Choux de Bruxelles Cavendish
Salade
Stilton-Cheddar
Soufflé glacé Alexandra
Chassagne Montrachet 1969
Château Latour 1959
Pol Roger
Dîner du   28 septembre

A Lucullan feast at the British Embassy, Paris.

After the degree ceremony, which took about two hours, we were taken by bus to the Ashmolean for tea and cakes and a spasm of culture. Then Mary and I returned to Hertford to dress for dinner. Again, I had to caparison myself in my scarlet robe.

Of the speeches at dinner, Bob McNamara's was the oddest and perhaps the most effective. He gave an account of how the Cuban missile crisis had nearly led to war. It was nothing to do with Oxford or academic life or those present at the dinner; but the topic clearly dominated his mind and he thought that it should stir us all. It did. He explained how he knew from his own experience at the time as Secretary of Defense that it had been touch and go whether the USA would intervene in Cuba with force. But what he did not know then but had learnt only recently was the readiness of the Soviets to meet force with force, with unimaginable consequences. Notwithstanding the flow of claret and the festive, candle-lit atmosphere of Balliol Hall where we were dining, McNamara's speech had a sobering effect on the company. We felt in some way that we had been made to feel how lucky we were, which we had not previously realised. I was called to speak after him and I can't say that the mood was propitious for an after-dinner speech such as I had carefully prepared. But I don't think that it would have gone down well even if it had not followed Bob's terrifying wake-up call. My moderate banter about Balliol met with frosty silence, which should not have surprised me as a good proportion of the company was from the college. Balliol had been instrumental, so I was told, in preventing Mrs Thatcher from getting an honorary doctorate at Oxford. Most of the Fellows had supported Heath rather than Jenkins for the university chancellorship, perhaps because he was the more vociferously anti-Maggie. Apart from this leavening of unsympathetic dons, some twenty Italians from the President's *entourage* were at the dinner. Even those who understood the language can't have grasped the inwardness of some of the remarks. When he came to wind up the proceedings Jenkins ran into the same mixture as I had done of ill-humour and incomprehension. I thought that he made a good speech but Balliol was not prepared to respond.

After it was all over in Balliol, Mary and I walked back in the rain to Hertford, where the Warnocks joined us for a post-mortem on the day's proceedings. I also took the opportunity of telling Geoffrey how much I was looking forward to his receiving a knighthood for his services to Oxford. In his dry way he retorted that Cicero preferred people to talk about why he had not been made a senator rather than why he had. He felt the same about an honour. Then, as we went to bed, I was conscious that I would have to live up to the honour of the doctorate that Oxford had bestowed on me, just as Mary and I would have to maintain the culinary standard with which the Public Orator had so eloquently identified us.

17

A MAN OF OUR TIMES

'I think you'd better be on time … and you'd better wear a dark suit and I don't know if you know that your tie's crooked.' It was Howard Davies[1] speaking. He was my private secretary in the British Embassy in Paris where, in 1975, I had just arrived as Ambassador and he was trying to get me on to the straight and narrow path of diplomacy in France. Feeling very new to it, I was ready for any instruction but I have to say that I was surprised to get it from Howard. I found it odd that he should be bothering about such things because I didn't think that the young minded about them (Howard was then twenty-four), least of all someone like Howard, whose background was far from patrician, and who was radically minded and unsympathetic to conventional au-

---

1 Sir Howard Davies, b. 1951; Chairman Financial Services Authority; m. 1984, Prudence Keely; Manchester Grammar School; Merton College, Oxford; a Harkness Fellow and graduate of Stanford Graduate School of Business, he served in the Treasury and the Foreign and Commonwealth Office, including two years as Private Secretary to the British Ambassador in Paris. Following appointment to McKinsey & Co. he became successively, Controller Audit Commission, Director General CBI, and Deputy-Governor Bank of England.

Howard Davies, cricketer.

thority. But, as I soon came to realise, Howard always wanted to make things work; and all that he was now doing was ensuring that the Embassy and its chief did not let the side down.

I will not endanger Howard's prospects by describing him here as the most brilliant man of his generation – a prognosis that often proves fatal. But he has undoubtedly carved out for himself a remarkable career and reputation in the public service and the City. His may not be a household name, but it is one to conjure with in financial circles. The organisation he now runs, the Financial Services Authority, will have more regulatory power than any comparable authority in the Western world.

However, the course he has followed has not been the one I would have predicted on the basis of the early picture I had formed of him. It is also dissimilar to the sort of vocation pursued by paragons of an earlier age who had the same kind of background as he has had. This reflects, I think, the complexity of his character and the changing nature of our times.

Long afterwards he told me, with unassuaged feelings of resentment, about an early experience he had when he first arrived at the Paris Embassy to serve as private secretary to my predecessor. The Ambassador was giving a large reception and asked Howard to assist by chatting with the guests and effecting the necessary introductions. 'Imagine my horror', Howard expostulated to me, 'when I looked at the guest-list and found that three-quarters of them were titled or belonged, or thought they did, to the *beau monde*.'

Fired by this painful memory of the *gratin*, Howard proceeded to say: 'And you were just as bad.' To my injured enquiry, he said: 'Yes, one day we were discussing what career I should pursue and whether the Foreign Service was really my scene – whether it would stretch me enough – and you said that you had once been posted as first secretary to the Embassy in Chile and that you did not have a great deal to do there but it didn't matter as you wrote a book.' Howard looked at me so indignantly that I asked him: 'What's wrong with that?' With some impatience he replied: 'The idea that one could be in a career where it didn't matter whether or not one was fully employed struck me as ridiculous.' I don't think he considered he was fully employed in the Embassy in Paris.

Those in the Chancery in Paris at the time who saw Howard at closer quarters than I did, both in and out of school, have told me of his unfailing cheerfulness and capacity for making work fun. He was always wonderful company and at his humorous best in preparing for ministerial or royal visits. He charmed the Queen Mother's *entourage* despite the initial misgivings of her private secretary, Martin Gilliat, who didn't think his platform-heeled shoes could belong to 'one of us'.

Although I would have been interested in it I was kept in the dark about Howard's technique with the girls, which was apparently confident and direct. History, as related to me, does not reveal how successful it was. A Lancashire lassie would be invited for a weekend in Paris and I heard tell of a jolly Australian girlfriend called 'Springy' (pronounced with a hard g), but my impression was that at this stage of his life his tastes were all-embracing. He began to lose his hair rather early. He seemed to bother little about his appearance. His manner was not exactly gracious. Yet he minded about his friendships and certainly had a winning way with him.

I asked him why ever he had joined the Foreign Service. He said that at Oxford he had found that it was regarded as the most difficult thing to get into. It was a challenge which he had to accept. He always had to test himself.

On several occasions in Paris, Howard and I discussed his future. I entirely accepted that diplomacy was not his *métier*, as he himself was increasingly coming to realise. But nor, apparently, was he tempted by left-wing politics. In this respect he differed from many of his counterparts of the thirties who, for understandable reasons, given the circumstances of the time, had been highly political and whose bookshelves had been crammed with the yellow-covered products of the Left Book Club. Like them, he had ideals, was on the side of the under-dog and wanted to do something useful. Unlike them, he had no faith in the possibility of setting the world to rights by the implementation of some comprehensive and ideological programme, involving widespread state intervention and political control. As Howard saw it, the trouble with institutions of the state was that they had not shown themselves to be sensitive to the market.

The market featured much in Howard's vocabulary. Some regulation was needed, but not control, let alone ownership, by the state. Phrases that had tripped so easily off the tongues of my contemporaries about the necessity for the Government to run and own the 'commanding heights of the economy' meant nothing to him.

By the mid-seventies Howard, along with many of his generation, was critical of what they saw as the hash being made by the political establishment in the running of the country. Whereas, in the sixties, the British had had some sort of claim, at any rate in the sphere of culture, to international leadership, a decade later they were renowned for being the 'sick man' of Europe. Unlike many of the young, however, Howard was not critical of the British Government's luke-warm attitude to the European Community. On the contrary, he was not far short of fanatical in his opposition to a 'yes' vote in the 1975 referendum. By the late nineties he had changed completely and I think it would be fair nowadays to call him a wholehearted European.

In our talks in Paris, Howard and I agreed that the Civil Service wouldn't do for him as a lifelong career. As someone who knows him well has expressed it, 'the words "servant" and "Howard" don't go well together'. I think that Howard at this stage of his life viewed government employment as too unadventurous, and as not providing enough scope for his organising aspirations. He is ambitious, as he is adaptable.

In any case, the pay in Whitehall was not all that good.

Howard is not possessed of expensive tastes, but, having no money at all of his own, he has had to make enough to ensure security. Focus on money ('it's not just my needs but those of my wife') is one of the ways in which, so it seems to me, the young of Howard's generation differ from those of my own. There are, of course, understandable reasons for it.

Howard was brought up in modest circumstances, the only child of a dominant mother and less dominant father. He is proud of the Manchester roots that still hold him, while he knows that he would not have blossomed fully had he not branched out at an early age.

As an undergraduate at Oxford he spent much of his leisure time in amateur dramatics. He would like to have been an actor, which would have satisfied the showman in him, but he didn't have the necessary qualities to command the stage. What he did have at this early phase of his life was a readiness to lead, a quality which he exercised with brio in theatrical circles at Oxford. It was in this milieu that he met the person who was to become one of his closest friends, Peter Stothard – who was later appointed Editor of *The Times* at about the same time as Howard was made Director General of the CBI. I doubt whether either expected when they were students that they would reach these particular heights simultaneously. I found it surprising to learn that as undergraduates they apparently never discussed politics together. But I should have remembered that, unlike my pre-war days at Oxford, politics did not then permeate student life.

If Howard, when a student or early in his career when I first met him, was not a political animal of the kind I was used to, he had definite views about the nature of society and government.

Like another Mancunian, A.J.P. Taylor, whom he resembled in some ways, he was not averse to being thought a bit of a 'bolshie', and to be seen to *épater les bourgeois*. He was in theory anti-establishment, even if he soon came to embody part of the establishment himself. As the years have gone by it is evident that he is committed to the work-ethic, disdains ostentation and hype and pays little heed to panache.

He does not relax easily and can give the impression of being driven. Yet to avoid giving too simple, too ascetic an outline of Howard's character, I have to stress that he enjoys the good things of life – the theatre, books, music and giving parties. He's a most attentive and original host. He frequently reviews novels and biographies, despite the other demands on his time. He reads regularly in bed at night. His favourite authors are Balzac, John Cowper Powys and Wyndham Lewis.

He has a network of friends, many of whom share his love of sport, which might be called the pivot of his pastimes. Whenever he can, and if not suffering from injury sustained on the field, he has over the years turned out to play in a regular six-a-side game of football organised originally by members of London Weekend Television. It takes place at midday on Fridays on a ground on the South Bank. It is impossible to exaggerate the competitiveness on the field of Howard and his friends, including rivalry over the incidence of injury. Howard apparently shows the same energy and determination to be at the heart of the game as he does to chase down foul play in the City. John Birt, a regular player in these matches, has had to carry him off the field three times as a result of injuries suffered in the fray. Greg Dyke, another in the same football league, is said to be particularly fast on the ball in the first half of the match.

Howard is an ardent supporter of Manchester City, a loyalty testifying to his sympathy, in sport as in politics, for the less-favoured. At matches, which he attends whenever possible, he will eschew the offer of a seat in the director's box and watch the game from the terraces, wearing a tweed cap. He is also a cricketer, playing regularly, not with television producers, but in a team largely made up of architects. The field is in Barnes. By accounts I have had, Howard is an all-rounder, equally vigorous with bat or ball, and pretty good at keeping an eye on the score-board.

He plays games with his two boys – whom he has sent to private schools for pragmatic reasons, because he doesn't think that state schools are good enough. Howard's devotion to his family is exemplary. 'The four of us have good times together,' his wife Prue told me. 'So you'd give him ten out of ten as a family man?' I asked her. 'Yes,' she said unhesitatingly, but then added, 'except for the washing-up.' He has no wish to live ostentatiously. Only recently has he acquired a second home of his own – in the West Country, where, to be sure, it would be contrary to all expectations if he took up hunting, shooting or even gardening.

Outside the home, in the various posts he has held in the public sector and the City, Howard has shown exceptional qualities as an inspector, regulator and organiser. After Paris and a spell at Stanford Graduate School, he transferred from the Foreign Service to the Treasury. He likes abroad and he loves foreign travel. Even so, the move was a natural progression, given his dislike of the social side of diplomatic life and his conviction that he was going to a seat of greater power.

He brought a spark to the Treasury where, early on, he dealt with the future of British Aerospace. In that capacity I recall him coming to Paris and our having a fierce argument over Britain's rejoining Airbus – which he was against. He was by nature more a Treasury than an FCO man. He fell in easily with the prevailing monetary policy, the discipline of which appealed to him. As Terry Burns, the Permanent Secretary to the Treasury, has put it to me, he was able 'to absorb and analyse a conglomeration of discordant facts and give them some sort of structure'. He had the skills of an official without behaving like one.

He was fond of pointing out inconsistencies and paradoxes. Those who worked with him soon became aware how low was his boredom threshold, yet he relished discussion and argument. He was no 'smoothie' and didn't fear to express unconventional opinions, or to mock and tease. His raillery was popular with the Treasury officials, and he just managed to avoid going too far. They saw him as something of a court jester but greatly admired his ability.

He left the Treasury to go to the consultancy firm, McKinsey, where the pay was higher. But then, in the middle of that appointment, he was called back to be special adviser to the Chancellor of the Exchequer, Nigel Lawson. This fitted in well with an idea that Howard was then toying with of entering politics in the Tory interest. He felt akin to Lawson politically and is credited with having helped in the drafting of some of his best speeches. He had a way of putting a gloss on the less popular issues.

But a chance came Howard's way that put the idea of a political career out of his mind. He was made Controller of the Audit Commission. The post might have been designed expressly for his training and talents which were making him very like the product of the Ecole Nationale d'Administration (ENA), the school established by de Gaulle in 1945 to produce people capable of running any part of French public life. (Howard is in fact sympathetic to everything French: their administration, their literature and – surprise, surprise – their food and wine.)

Set up by Michael Heseltine, the Audit Commission had been given far-reaching responsibility for checking the expenditure and efficiency of local government in England and Wales. Howard managed to get its coverage extended to the National Health Service. As chairman of this enlarged organisation, he brought to the task of inspection some of the qualities of both Scrooge and Sherlock Holmes. He emerged triumphant one day, for instance, when, after detective work on the financial affairs of the police, he was able to prove that their heavy expenditure on fingerprints was not remotely justified by the number of cases in which these had helped to lead to a conviction. John Banham, who was his predecessor as chairman of the Commission, has described him in this role as 'a great communicator'. He became a regular performer on *Question Time* and *Any Questions* and revealed that he had a special gift for explaining difficult issues to the general public, readily and concisely, and often with a touch of humour.

He left the Audit Commission for what proved to be a much less interesting post, Director General of the CBI. He was not his own master, but the post did at least provide him with a platform where he was able to develop his reputation for being an authoritative speaker on public affairs without being a politician. He stayed there three years.

The offer then made to him of the deputy-governorship of the Bank of England came as a way of escape from the travails of the

CBI. He made a success of the Bank, instigating badly needed administrative reforms, which was an Augean task after his own heart. The flunkeys soon became fewer.

This satisfactory period in Howard's life came to a sudden end when Gordon Brown, on becoming Chancellor of the Exchequer, declared that the Bank would henceforth be independent of the Government and that it would have two deputy-governors, instead of one, as hitherto. It was also going to be deprived of its regulatory functions, which were to be assigned to a new independent authority. Nobody at the Bank had been consulted about these major changes. Howard, who happened to be in Buenos Aires at the time, felt that his nose had been put out of joint. Why did there have to be a second deputy-governor? Eddie George, the Governor, was also upset, and Threadneedle Street was in turmoil. The Old Lady sensed, not so much that she had been raped, but – almost as bad – that she had been ignored.

The crisis was only resolved by Terry Burns and Howard getting together in a rescue operation that sorely tested their endurance and ingenuity. The outcome involved a major and hazardous commitment by Howard, who agreed to become the Executive Chairman of the new Financial Services Authority (FSA), the City's all-powerful financial regulator.

He has described his role as being 'the City's plain-clothes policeman' but in fact he not only has to control crime, but to help in the avoidance of unnecessary risks by financial customers – City-speak for individual investors, holders of private insurance, pensions or of any financial instruments. These people, perhaps amounting now to more than twenty million, are operating in a changed financial environment governed by totally new technology. The previous system, based on self-regulation, had proved ineffective, as shown, for example, by the collapse of Barings or the Maxwell pensions scandal. Howard has had to weld together into a single private-sector company, with a staff of over two thousand, ten different regulatory bodies.

As I considered Howard's career I couldn't help thinking that this appointment sounded very unlike the sort of activity I had foreseen for him when, earlier, we had discussed his future; and I asked myself whether it really suited him. I decided to see him about it. We met in the impressive and sparklingly new premises of the FSA at Canary Wharf. We sat in the corner of a vast open plan office and, over coffee, I expressed surprise that his career had led him to this particular pinnacle. He replied in his usual calm, matter-of-fact way: 'No, well, I didn't plan it quite like this. As you know Gordon Brown reorganised the Bank of England where I was Deputy-Governor, and it was decided that I should come here.'

He then shifted into a more sentient vein, saying: 'But I must tell you that I get great satisfaction from it, from the responsibility that the FSA has taken on to prevent people being exploited and to make the financial markets work.' During the long passage through Parliament of the bill setting up the FSA, concern was expressed there and in the City about the concentration of so much power in Howard's hands; and he is bound to run into criticism as he proceeds to knit together all the present regulatory organisations. But I am sure he will be able to stand up to it. My worry is rather different. As I hinted to him personally, I could not help wondering how far certain facets of his character – his creativity, his love of the arts, his informality and his gift for public exposition – were going to find fulfilment in life in the City, however exalted. He began to talk again rapidly about the statutory obligations of his organisation and I became convinced that, for the time being at any rate, he had found gratification in the unprecedented responsibility of making something quite new and highly important work in the interests of the well-being of the country. Making things work had always been the leitmotif of his life, as I knew from my first contact with him many years before in Paris.

18

THE LOVELOCKS

The Arab pony stood looking over the fence into the Combe churchyard as the family and the rest of the congregation followed Mrs Lovelock's coffin up the grassy slope, past ancient tombstones, before it was lowered into the grave. 'Earth to earth,' intoned the Rector. The November sun lit up the mourners and gilded the tops of the downs opposite. 'Resurrection to eternal life,' the Rector continued. The pony twitched its ears. When the time came for us all to turn away from her grave and disperse down the hill, half-suppressed sobs and the sound of her son-in-law's trumpet composed our elegy.

Mrs Lovelock died in 1992. She had been the pillar of our village, Combe, in the Berkshire Downs, since she and her husband, Herbert, moved there from Wexcombe during the war. His work had been to meet the country's needs for increased food production by reclaiming hundreds of acres of downland covered with scrub and gorse, which had hitherto been devoted to shooting. I remember scrabbling about there bird-watching as a child when my parents had a cottage over the hill at Inkpen. Herbert Lovelock

*Florence and Herbert
Lovelock.*

cleared the land with the help, ironical though it may sound (not, I am sure, that Herbert gave its provenance a thought) of a German caterpillar tractor, called for political correctness a Bulldog. The only way the machine could be started was by exploding a cartridge inserted deep into the engine.

After the war Herbert was given charge of a herd of cows, which provided the mainstay of the village's economy. Mrs Lovelock brought up a family of five children. The youngest, a boy, was born long after the others and, to avoid him having a lonely childhood, Mrs Lovelock became the foster-parent of another boy.

Life for the Lovelock family in those days was rough and simple. But they were never short of meat. Herbert always carried a gun on his tractor and there was plenty of game about, and no keepers. 'Mum's rabbit pies were something,' Joan, her eldest daughter, told me many years later, licking her lips. I asked Joan what she and her brothers and sister and, for that matter also, her father and mother, did for recreation during, and in the early years after, the war. At that time, she reminded me, there was no electricity, and no bus service or pub at Combe, nor, of course, any TV. Country people, she believed, were more affected than nowadays by the frequent and unpredictable changes in the weather; but also, perhaps, they were more aware of the alternating beauty of the scenery. 'On Sunday afternoons in the summer', she said, 'we all put on our best clothes and went for a walk.' When I asked 'Where to?' she answered: 'Oh, to Faccombe or Inkpen' (neighbouring villages). She added: 'In winter we played games on Sundays and did a lot of cheating.' Occasionally there was a bicycle outing to the cinema in Andover. As there was no electricity, one of the treats in the evening was to get hold of a torch, scramble into bed and read under the blankets.

In the absence of a bathroom, Mrs Lovelock presided on Friday nights over a copper tub that was hauled into the living-room in front of the kitchen range, where they all took their turn to bathe. Her supervision of this ritual symbolised her control over the family. There was nothing overbearing about her. It was an accepted matter of course that she looked after everyone and everything. She never seemed to be in a hurry. Wearing spectacles and of medium height, she was always neatly turned out for work in well-ironed floral dresses, beneath blue aprons. She loved pink, and on Sundays wore a blouse of that colour and earrings to match. In later years she paid regular visits to the hairdresser in Kintbury, called Teasers. Herbert, in contrast, was a large burly man who left to her the day-to-day running of the family. Not much given to small talk, whenever he saw us in the village he would stop and ask: 'How's things going at the School House?' He had a deep and ready laugh. He moved steadily but slowly about his business. He personified imperturbability.

They lived in Box Cottage, a square two-up-and-two-down brick and flint house, with roses, sweet peas and clematis climbing up the walls. Mrs Lovelock appeared ready to feed all comers. Children, dogs, birds and hedgehogs seemed to know instinctively that they were all welcome and would all be able to find their favourite delicacy. Saucers were strewn everywhere.

Having moved to Combe, Mrs Lovelock devoted herself for the next half-century to her new home, her family and the welfare of everyone in the village. She helped the Fosburys in their shop and bakery. These were still flourishing when we arrived in Combe in 1961. Mrs Fosbury ran the shop, writing down the orders one by one as the customer gave them, putting the price against them down to the last farthing, and then fetching each item one by one from the shelves and placing it on the counter – an unhurried process that allowed plenty of time for waiting customers to exchange the latest news of the village. It was the very model of a non-supermarket. We all had accounts there, including our beagle dog. When we moved to Spain in the mid-sixties we left him with the Jellicoes at Tidcombe, which was situated some half-dozen miles away. He used to make his way regularly by himself over the downs to Combe, and, not finding us there, he would go to the shop where he was given biscuits on his account before Mrs Fosbury telephoned the Jellicoes to come to fetch him back. Alas, this shopping spree, which had gone on for many years, came to a sad and violent end one day, when, somewhere on his journey to Combe, he was run over and killed.

At Combe, which is only seventy miles from London, the pattern of life has remained idyllically unchanged. The village is situated far from the main road, six hundred feet up and surrounded by chalk downs. It is liable to be cut off by snow in winter – which, it has to be said, some find more romantic than others. The resistance we have maintained to all attempts to improve our accessibility to the outside world has been boosted by the existence in the valley of the stone curlew. At least the ornithologists claim that this is one of their few surviving habitats, and the plenitude of flints in the region lends support to the idea, though alas I can't personally vouch for their presence.

One feature of the landscape, and one event associated with its local history, confound the impression of eternal calm and rural bliss. A gibbet stands at the top of the hill separating Combe from the village of Inkpen on the other side. Once upon a time a poor widow living at Combe with two sons fell in love with a man living over the downs, and he with her. He was a carrier and used to travel several times a week with his cart to deliver parcels to Combe. But he had a wife and could not therefore marry the widow. So he decided to murder his wife. Accordingly, he enticed her to go on a journey with him, and on the way he persuaded her to get out of the cart and to look at something in a thicket beside the road. In fact, what he wanted to do was to lead her into a nest of hornets. His plan worked and he flung her down in the middle of the swarm, where she was then stung to death.

That evening he went and told the widow what he had done. Unknown to him, one of the widow's two sons, who was in bed in the room next door, overheard what he said. The next morning he related it to a neighbouring farmer. The man and woman were arrested and convicted of murder. She was regarded as an accomplice in the crime. They were sentenced to be hanged in the parish where the murder had been committed. But that was not the end of the story. A quarrel broke out between the villages of Combe and Inkpen about where exactly the crime had taken place. Neither wished to bear the cost of the execution. In the end, as neither parish would yield, higher authority was sought and it was decided that a gibbet should be erected on the boundary line between the two parishes, and the cost borne equally by both.

The execution proved to be a great public occasion, attended by a concourse of people from all walks of life, arriving on foot, on horseback or by coach. Much food and drink was consumed. The crowd was hilarious and boasted that there would never be a greater 'picnic' on the beacon. It was not long before the murderers, who were hanging in chains from the gibbet, provided a feast for the ravens, crows and falcons. The gibbet survives to this day, though there have been no more hangings.

From the time when we settled at Combe, Mrs Lovelock became our cleaner, housekeeper and watchdog. She was an indispensable part of our life. She was completely charmed by Mary and even persuaded herself that she looked like the Queen. She felt as close to my daughter, Alexandra, and her children as to her own family. For birthdays and Christmas she knitted them pullovers decorated with birds or animals to match each individual taste. She told them where the new nests were to be found and how many eggs had been laid. She warned them where the traps lay that had been set for the mice, and proudly related the quantity caught since they had last met.

We lived abroad for many years and throughout that time she kept us informed by regular correspondence of everything we needed to know about our house and garden as well as about the gossip of the village. She proved to be a marvellous letter-writer. She wrote to us when we were living in Madrid to report that Mr and Mrs Fosbury had presented her with a gold wristwatch for her many years' work in the shop: 'I was overwhelmed but I am not making it public as there are some real sarcastic people who would make something of it if they knew. The woods and lanes are now yellow with primroses and the violets are popping up so you can imagine what Combe is looking like.' Another letter reported: 'There is an owl in your garden nights making the most high pitch screech. Mr Bennett has put the toilet right and the leak in the pipe was where the cistern was filling up.' We were kept abreast of the wildlife, thus: 'The squirrels have eaten all the walnuts also I have caught two fat mice in the cottage and two in the school.'

One Easter when we were abroad and Alexandra was alone at the cottage, Mrs Lovelock felt so sorry for her that she brought her a tray with a three-course meal that she had specially cooked. Alexandra, then an undergraduate, gave a Fifth of November fireworks party and dance one year for her friends from Oxford. She invited the Lovelocks, who assumed the role of alternative parents, seated silently at the edge of the room and keeping an eye on everyone. Afterwards, we received a letter from Mrs Lovelock describing it all – the dresses and the dancing – in graphic detail such as the *Tatler* would have been proud to publish.

Mrs Lovelock took it upon herself to look after the Combe church and ensure that it was clean, the altar full of flowers, usually from her own garden, and the brass cross and candlesticks always kept shining. She never complained that she was tired or sought a lift up the hill to the church.

One other unforgettable gift Mrs Lovelock brought to us and our village was her singing. In the church she was a choir in herself. The sudden absence of her voice in the funeral service at Combe on that November afternoon, with which I began this brief word-picture, was a poignant reminder of what we had all lost.

Not Heaven itself upon the past has power;
But what has been, has been, and I have had my hour.

From Dryden's translation of an ode by Horace

INDEX WITH NOTES

Old Friends and Modern Instances

later DBE, d. of 2nd Baron
Redesdale; served WW2 Coldstream
Guards; politician; race-horse owner
and Steward of the Jockey Club; art-
patron and philanthropist; author of
Park Top: a romance of the Turf. The
Duchess manages the estate and,
following the literary bent of her
family, has written about the house
and garden 123, 137–43
Dowler, David (1931–70), Civil Servant;
Principal Private Secretary to Roy
Jenkins at Ministry of Civil
Aviation, Home Office and Treasury,
the last jointly with Robert
Armstrong 91
Drury, Martin (b.1938), Director-
General National Trust; m. Elizabeth
Bridgeman 148
Dyke, Gregory (b. 1947), since 2000
Director-General BBC; formerly
Editor in Chief, TV am; Director of
Programmes and later Managing
Director London Weekend
Television 148

E
Ecole Nationale d'Administration
(ENA), school established by de
Gaulle in 1945 to prepare people to
run the political, economic and
industrial life of the country 188
Elizabeth, the Queen Mother 26

F
Fermor, Patrick Leigh, DSO, OBE (b.
1915), m. Joan Eyres-Monsell; served
WW2 in Greece and Crete; soldier,
traveller and author 123, 141
Financial Services Authority 179
Fleming, Ann, née Charteris, see ftn.
p.117, 48, 91, 95, 117–25

Forbes, Alastair (b. 1918), journalist
famed for his labyrinthine style 91
Foster, Roy (b.1949), Carroll Professor
of Irish History, Oxford, since 1991;
has written several highly acclaimed
biographies 59
Fox, Sir Paul, CBE (b. 1925), war
service, Parachute Regiment; TV
scriptwriter, editor and director;
Controller and Director of
Programmes BBC; Channel Four;
World TV News; Thames TV
58
Franks, Oliver, Baron, OM, GCMG,
KCB, KCVO (1905–92), don,
government administrator,
ambassador and banker, see ftn.
p.81, 63, 81–90
Fraser, Rt. Hon. Sir Hugh, MBE
(1918–84), war service with Lovat
Scouts, Phantom and Special Air
Service; politician, Tory MP; m.
Lady Antonia Pakenham; Secretary
of State for Air 74
Freeman, Rt.Hon. John (b. 1915),
Labour MP, journalist, diplomat and
businessman; Ed. *New Statesman*
1961–5; British High Commissioner
to India 1965–8; Ambassador to USA
1969–71; Chairman Independent TV
News; Professor of International
Relations, University of California
58
Fry, Roger (1866–1934), painter and art
critic 3, 47

G
Gaitskell, Rt. Hon. Hugh (1906–63),
politician, Labour MP; m. Dora
Creditor, later Baroness Gaitskell;
Minister of Fuel and Power;
Minister of State for Economic

206

Index With Notes

Roll, Eric, Baron, KCMG, CB (b. 1907), banker, economist, government administrator and author 85

Rose, Jim, CBE (1909–99), m. Susan Pamela Gibson; Chairman Penguin Books; Literary Editor, *Observer*; Director, International Press Institute, Zurich; *Survey of Race Relations in Britain 1963–69* 148

Rothschild, Jacob, Baron, GBE (b. 1936), financier and art-patron; m. Serena Dunn; Chairman National Gallery; Chairman National Heritage Memorial Fund; Chairman Five Arrows; RIT Capital Partners 45

Rowse, A. L., CH (1903–99), historian; Emeritus Fellow of All Souls College Oxford; published numerous works particularly concerning Cornwall, Shakespeare, poetry and English history 153, 154

Roxburgh, J. F. (1885–1954), Headmaster of Stowe School from its foundation; subject of biography by Noël Annan who wrote of his aim to change much in the traditional public school order, 'he wanted the school to be less dominated by the worship of games and less regimented' 39

Runciman, Hon. Sir Steven, CH (b. 1903), don, author and historian, notably of Byzantium; Fellow of Trinity College Cambridge 44

Rylands, George, known as Dadie, CH (1902–98), don, theatre director, literary critic and author; Fellow of King's College, Cambridge 6, 40, 41, 43

S

Schlesinger, Arthur (b. 1917), American writer and historian; Emeritus Professor of Humanities, City University of New York 172

Schmidt, Helmut (b. 1918), German economist and politician; member of Social Democrat Party since 1946; Federal Chancellor 1974–82 102

Selwoods, a family living near Bristol, many of whom worked for members of the Bloomsbury Group 6

Souter- Robertson, Joan (1903–94), painter; m. Jean Cochemé 21, 22

Sparrow, John (1906–99), served WW2 Coldstream Guards and War Office; barrister; Warden of All Souls College, Oxford, 1952–77, won Chancellor's Prize for Latin Verse; literary reviewer, essayist and anthologist 123, 154, 155

Stephen, Ann and Judith, daughters of Dr Adrian Stephen and Dr. Karen Costelloe, both psychoanalysts; he was the younger brother of Vanessa and Virginia 7

Stirling, Sir David, DSO, OBE (1915–90), served WW2 Scots Guards, No 3 Commando (Brig. of Guards), First SAS Regt.; POW. President Capricorn Africa Society; Chairman Television International Enterprises 108, 109

Stothard, Peter (b.1951), Editor of *The Times* since 1992 184

Strachey, Giles Lytton (1880–1932), author; s. of Sir Richard Strachey, see ftn. p.1, 1, 2, 8, 11–16 *passim*, 23–5

Strachey, James (1887–1967), translator of the works of Sigmund Freud, m. Alix Sargent-Florence 18

Strachey, Marjorie (1882–1964), teacher, see ftn. p.1, 1–6

Old Friends and Modern Instances